THIS BOOK BELONGS TO

If found, please return to

_____

_____

FEAST

A 3-MONTH JOURNEY TO BECOMING
A WELL-FED WOMAN

———

from Rachel W. Cole

COPYRIGHT © 2016 RACHEL W. COLE

Cover design, interior layout, and illustrations by Chelsey Dyer

All rights reserved. You, the purchaser, may use this workbook for your own personal development, but no part of this publication may be reproduced, distributed, or transmitted in any form or by any means, including photocopying, recording, or other electronic or mechanical methods, without the prior written permission of the author. In the case of brief quotations embodied in critical reviews and certain other noncommercial uses permitted by copyright law please contact the author at rachel@rachelwcole.com with the header "*FEAST* REFERENCE REQUEST" for permission.

DISCLAIMER

Although every precaution has been taken to verify the accuracy of the information contained herein, the author assumes no responsibility for any errors or omissions. No liability is assumed for damages that may result from the use of information contained within.

By reading and/or utilizing this workbook and enrolling in the *Feast* program you acknowledge that I, Rachel W Cole, am not a licensed psychologist or health care professional and my services do not replace the care of psychologists or other healthcare professionals. Coaching, teaching, and the writings I share are in no way to be construed or substituted as psychological counseling or any other type of therapy or medical advice. I will at all times exercise my best professional efforts, skills and care. However, I cannot guarantee the outcome of coaching or teaching efforts and/or recommendations and my comments about the outcome are expressions of opinion only. I cannot make any guarantees other than to deliver the services purchased as described.

TABLE OF CONTENTS

PREFACE

Introduction	10
Your *Feast* Calendar	16
Are you ready?	20

THE FOUNDATION

WEEK ONE: SELF-COMPASSION

Lesson	24
Reflections	30
Challenges	32
Expert Interview Bio — Kristin Neff	34
Daily Practice Checklist	38

WEEK TWO: CARING FOR YOUR SENSITIVE SOUL

Lesson	42
Reflections	48
Challenges	50
Expert Interview Bio — Kate Read	51
Daily Practice Checklist	54

WEEK THREE: EFFECTIVE EMOTIONAL COPING

Lesson	58
Reflections	63
Challenges	69
Expert Interview Bio — Signe Darpinian	74
Daily Practice Checklist	77

WEEK FOUR: INTEGRATION WEEK

Tips for taking advantage of Integration Week	82
Reading Reflection Questions	83
The Health at Every Size Manifesto by Linda Bacon	88

AT THE TABLE

Setting the Table	98

WEEK FIVE: HONORING HUNGER & FULLNESS

Lesson	102
Reflections	107
Challenges	110
Expert Interview Bio — Tracy Brown	112
Daily Practice Checklist	116

WEEK SIX: EATING FREELY

Lesson	122
Reflections	126
Challenges	128
Expert Interview Bio — Dana & Hilary	132
Daily Practice Checklist	135

WEEK SEVEN: PLEASURE & SATISFACTION

Lesson	140
Reflections	144
Challenges	147
Expert Interview Bio — Carmen Cool	148
Daily Practice Checklist	152

WEEK EIGHT: JOYFUL MOVEMENT

Lesson	158
Reflections	162
Challenges	164
Expert Interview Bio — Anna Guest-Jelley & Rachel Marcus)	166
Daily Practice Checklist	171

WEEK NINE: INTEGRATION WEEK
"Walk Slowly" by Dana Faulds   178

LIVING A WELL-FED LIFE

WEEK TEN: BECOMING A WELL-FED WOMAN / PART I
Lesson	184
Reflections	191
Challenges	194
Resource Folder Interviewee Bios	195
Daily Practice Checklist	202

WEEK ELEVEN: BECOMING A WELL-FED WOMAN / PART II
Lesson	210
Reflections	214
Challenges	215
Daily Practice Checklist	219

WEEK TWELVE: CLOSING, CELEBRATION, AND WHAT'S NEXT?
You did enough.	228
Reflections	230
Challenges	234
Suggested Reading List	236
Good People to Know and Follow	238
Blank Daily Practice Checklist	240

ABOUT RACHEL   247

LOVE AFTER LOVE

The time will come
when, with elation
you will greet yourself arriving
at your own door, in your own mirror
and each will smile at the other's welcome,

and say, sit here. Eat.
You will love again the stranger who was your self.
Give wine. Give bread. Give back your heart
to itself, to the stranger who has loved you

all your life, whom you ignored
for another, who knows you by heart.
Take down the love letters from the bookshelf,

the photographs, the desperate notes,
peel your own image from the mirror.
Sit. *Feast on your life.*

— DEREK WALCOTT

THE WORKBOOK EXPERIMENT

For the past year, I have run *Feast* delivering the content digitally. Lessons were distributed via email. Worksheets were PDF documents students could print at home. This approach worked but some students wanted a physical workbook with materials all in one place. They wanted preprinted materials. They wanted an easy way to take *Feast* with them to a favorite cafe, to dive deep with a mug of their favorite coffee.

My fear in offering a workbook rather than digitally 'dripping' the content one day at a time, has been that students would skip ahead and be overwhelmed by what's to come. I believe *Feast* works best when one focuses only on the present topic. Please use this workbook with this in mind.

Ultimately, I concluded the potential advantages of a printed workbook outweigh the potential drawbacks, so the *Feast* Workbook was born. You are the first *Feast* students to use this workbook; I'll be eager to learn what your experience with it is like.

Using the workbook is entirely optional, as course materials will still arrive each week by email. You will be able to choose whichever system works best for you.

AN OVERVIEW OF THE *FEAST* EXPERIENCE

BUDDY PAIRINGS

You have the option to be paired with a fellow *Feast* student for the duration of the course. The benefit of having a buddy is that you will have the opportunity for more support, accountability, and connection and, importantly, it may enhance your learning. The exact buddy pairing arrangements is unique to each pairing. As buddies, you would co-design the experience that is most useful and comfortable, including how frequently you would connect (once weekly, twice weekly, etc.), using what medium (telephone, Skype, texting, email, etc.), and how you would take advantage of each other's support.

Again, pairing up is optional, however, many people find it very helpful. If you would like to have a buddy, please let Rachel know by the first week of *Feast*.

THE PRIVATE FACEBOOK GROUP

Facebook certainly has its downsides and some of you may not yet be well versed in this platform. However it's actually quite easy and, for now, the best way for us to stay connected throughout the week. Our group will be entirely private – anything you post can be accessed only by group members. We will use our Facebook group to discuss the course learnings and to share questions, challenges, and celebrations.

Feast's Facebook group conduct guidelines:

1. **NO NUMBERS.** Please don't share how many cookies you ate, what you weigh, how long you spent on the treadmill. Numbers don't matter, they are triggers for some people and can incite unhelpful comparison.

2. **CONFIDENTIALITY.** Everything shared within the group is confidential. No sharing with anyone outside of our group. No exceptions. Period.

3. **SHARE FROM YOUR OWN EXPERIENCE.** Instead of giving advice or trying to solve someone else's challenge, share from your own experiences. For example "In my experience, taking ten deep breaths before I go into the kitchen really helps me to slow things down" instead of "Have you thought about taking ten deep breaths before you go into the kitchen? That might help slow things down for you."

INTUITIVE EATING, THE BOOK

Beginning week three you will be asked to begin reading *Intuitive Eating* (3rd edition). The material in this book is an essential and valuable part of the learning. Please plan to stay on top of your reading assignments. You will notice we will read the book out of order, tracking *Feast* learnings. The assignments are as follows

WEEK 3: CHAPTER 11
WEEK 4: FORWARD – CHAPTER 5 AND CHAPTER 7
WEEK 5: CHAPTERS 6 AND 9
WEEK 6: CHAPTER 8
WEEK 7: CHAPTER 10
WEEK 8: CHAPTERS 12 AND 13

ONE-ON-ONE TIME WITH RACHEL

Students who applied to *Feast* by the early bird deadline receive a complimentary 45-minute, one-on-one session with Rachel to be used at any time before the course ends. PLEASE NOTE: You must schedule and complete your complimentary session before the end of the course otherwise you forfeit the session.

Whether you received one of these bonus sessions or not, you may find yourself wanting some additional support and attention. If so, you may book a 45-minute session for an additional $100.

To schedule, please visit: *https://calendly.com/rachelcole/Feast*

DAILY PRACTICE CHECKLISTS

Each week you'll be provided a daily practice checklist. It includes the new skills we will learn that week and, after the first week, the skills learned in previous weeks.

The daily practices are available because It is easy to accumulate this new knowledge but not put it into practice. The checklists are here to help you turn learning into change.

That said, it's very important this chart not be used as a weapon to judge or shame. Rather, it should be used as a place to celebrate yourself each time you make a choice to care and feed yourself.

The goal is not to get as many gold stars as possible. I repeat: the goal is not to get as many gold stars as possible. You are not being asked to use every skill every day. You are being asked to use new skills if and when you need them.

The chart is not a tool for guilt or striving or weight loss. It is a tool for kindness and support. The goal is simply to notice and acknowledge when you have used a new skill or showed up to participate in *Feast* and your life.

If you find this chart triggering or unhelpful, *don't use it*. It's only there to be helpful.

To use it, simply scan through the skills listed and reflect: "Did I use any of these skills today?" If you did, put a star or a heart or a smiley face. That's it. If there is a skill you want to track that you do not see included, use the blank lines at the end of each section to customize this chart.

Again, the chart is totally optional and will work great for some, but not all, people.

INTEGRATION WEEKS

Weeks four and nine are integration weeks. Aside from a reading assignment during week four, you have no specific responsibilities during these weeks. These weeks offer you a chance to breathe, digest, and ponder your *Feast* journey.

My advice for moving forward during integration weeks is to make time to review the material:

1. Take this workbook with you to your favorite cafe and make a date for reflecting on it, rereading and journaling about what we have covered thus far.
2. Schedule a review session with your buddy if you have one.
3. PRACTICE. PRACTICE. PRACTICE. Use your new skills. It's okay to be awkward with them. Practice anyway. Practice at work. Practice with your friends and families. Practice.

THE WEEKLY SCHEDULE

While most of the material you need is already inside this workbook, there is still pace that we'll go through things.

> SUNDAYS
> A new audio meditation for the week
>
> MONDAYS
> A written lesson on the week's theme
>
> TUESDAYS
> Journal inquiries and self-reflections
>
> WEDNESDAYS
> Select challenges and activities to put learning into action
>
> THURSDAYS
> An audio interview featuring a conversation with a guest expert
> Live call with Rachel for discussion, troubleshooting and support
> (at 9:00 a.m. or 4:00 p.m. PST)

FINAL PREPARATIONS

If you're ready, here are some things you can do to prepare:

1. Purchase your copy of *Intuitive Eating* (3rd Edition).
2. Set aside time each morning, evening, and/or weekends to engage with *Feast* materials and practices. If needed, inform your family that this is sacred time when you will be unavailable.
3. Review the course calendar and enter into your personal calendar the live calls you plan to attend. The calls are every Thursday at 9 am and 4 pm PST. There are no live calls during our integration weeks.
4. If you have one, reach out to your buddy to connect and design your commitments.
5. Join the Facebook group.
6. Watch the welcome video.
7. Reflect on your intentions for this journey. Get as clear as you can about your commitment. Perhaps, pick one word to anchor you as we head out. It might be 'vulnerability' or 'possibility', ... consider what word is at the heart of how you want to step into our *Feast* circle.

A final note before we depart…

You might think I regret my eating disorder. You might think I look back in shame at all the seemingly wasted energy I spent obsessing about the number on the scale or the food on my plate.

But I don't have shame.

Instead I have compassion and a deep awareness that, at that time, I was taking care of myself the very best way that I knew how.

At the time, I was in pain and I was anxious, both of which declined when I focused intensely on food and my body.

I actually think 20-year-old me was pretty resourceful.

Yes, she was also miserable, ill, and hungry. But she was, nevertheless, resourceful, using her limited toolbox as best she could.

As the old adage goes: when you know better, you do better.

I frequently encounter women who feel such self-loathing for all the years spent riding the diet pendulum, abusing alcohol, or overspending.

However you cope, it is or was most certainly you taking care of yourself the best way you know or knew how.

I believe that when you know a better way you do it.

Regardless, whatever your salve, self-care is often mislabeled as self-harm and I want to change that.

Let's forgive ourselves for the hurt our efforts to help ourselves caused.

Let's celebrate that when we're hurting our natural tendency is to take care of ourselves by any means necessary. (Look in the mirror; you will see someone who has, all along, been on your team).

And finally, once we've forgiven and seen the goodness of our true nature, we can move towards the discovery of effective, less-harmful self-care methods.

If it's time for you to make your toolbox more robust…

If you're ready for the resilient life that comes after you forgive yourself…

If you understand that being a sensitive soul comes with a different life-playbook…

If stepping fully into the roles of advocate, soft-place-to-fall, ally, lover, champion, and oxygen-giver for yourself is what you're called to do…

I invite you to *Feast*.

Rachel

CALENDAR

DAILY: Listen to guided meditation, participate in the Facebook group, and practice new skills.

	DATE	WEEKLY TOPIC	ACTIVITY OR EVENT
WEEK 1	8/1	Self-Compassion	Read the week's lesson
	8/2	Self-Compassion	Complete assessments and journal inquiries
	8/3	Self-Compassion	Complete challenge or activity
	8/4	Becoming a Well-fed Woman, Part II	Listen to expert interview; Live Call, 9am and 4pm PST

	DATE	WEEKLY TOPIC	ACTIVITY OR EVENT
WEEK 2	8/8	Caring for the Sensitive Soul	Read the week's lesson
	8/9	Caring for the Sensitive Soul	Complete assessments and journal inquiries
	8/10	Caring for the Sensitive Soul	Complete challenge or activity
	8/11	Caring for the Sensitive Soul	Listen to expert interview; Live Call, 9am and 4pm PST

	DATE	WEEKLY TOPIC	ACTIVITY OR EVENT
WEEK 3	8/15	Caring for the Sensitive Soul	Read the week's lesson
	8/16	Caring for the Sensitive Soul	Complete assessments and journal inquiries
	8/17	Caring for the Sensitive Soul	Complete challenge or activity
	8/18	Caring for the Sensitive Soul	Listen to expert interview; Live Call, 9am and 4pm PST

Read pages 149–165 (Chapter 11) in Intuitive Eating

	DATE	WEEKLY TOPIC	
WEEK 4	8/22	Integration Week	

Read pages 1–58 (Forward – Chapter 5 and 74–93 (Chapter 7) in Intuitive Eating

CALENDAR

DATE	WEEKLY TOPIC	ACTIVITY OR EVENT
9/19	Joyful Movement	Read the week's lesson
9/20	Joyful Movement	Complete assessments and journal inquiries
9/21	Joyful Movement	Complete challenge or activity
9/22	Joyful Movement	Listen to expert interview; Live Call, 9am and 4pm PST

Read pages 167–195 (Chapters 12 and 13) in Intuitive Eating

WEEK 8

DATE	WEEKLY TOPIC	ACTIVITY OR EVENT
9/26	Integration Week	

WEEK 9

DATE	WEEKLY TOPIC	ACTIVITY OR EVENT
10/3	Becoming a Well-fed Woman, Part I	Read the week's lesson
10/4	Becoming a Well-fed Woman, Part I	Complete assessments and journal inquiries
10/5	Becoming a Well-fed Woman, Part I	Complete challenge or activity
10/6	Becoming a Well-fed Woman, Part I	Listen to expert interview; Live Call, 9am and 4pm PST

WEEK 10

DATE	WEEKLY TOPIC	ACTIVITY OR EVENT
10/10	Honoring Hunger & Fullness	Read the week's lesson
10/11	Honoring Hunger & Fullness	Complete assessments and journal inquiries
10/12	Honoring Hunger & Fullness	Complete challenge or activity
10/13	Honoring Hunger & Fullness	Listen to expert interview; Live Call, 9am and 4pm PST

WEEK 11

DATE	WEEKLY TOPIC	ACTIVITY OR EVENT
10/17	Integration & Closing Ceremony	TBD
10/18	Integration & Closing Ceremony	TBD
10/19	Integration & Closing Ceremony	TBD
10/20	Integration & Closing Ceremony	Listen to expert interview; Live Call, 9am and 4pm PST

WEEK 12

Once-monthly live group calls with other Feast alums after the course ends for support, accountability, and on-the-spot coaching.

Curious if you're ready to embark on the *Feast* journey?

My guess is that you are ready but if you want to see for sure, use these checklists to assure yourself.

OUTER READINESS CHECKLIST

- ☐ I've purchased my copy of *Intuitive Eating* (3rd Edition)
- ☐ I have reviewed the course calendar.
- ☐ I have scheduled the live calls I plan to attend into my personal calendar
- ☐ I've noted in my calendar which weeks are integration weeks and have no live calls.
- ☐ I've set aside some time each morning, evening, and/or weekend to engage with *Feast* materials and practices. If needed, I've informed my family that this is sacred time where I will be unavailable.
- ☐ I've let Rachel know if I want buddy.
- ☐ I've joined the Facebook group and introduced myself in a comment below Rachel's call for introductions.
- ☐ I've watched the welcome video.
- ☐ I've gathered or identified physical supports for the journey:
    - ☐ A nice journal and pen
    - ☐ A cozy place to sit for journaling, the live-calls, and meditation
    - ☐ A special mug to drink my favorite beverage from
    - ☐ A sacred candle to burn
    - ☐ My '*Feast*' necklace (If you don't currently have this it's in the mail!)
    - Other:

INNER READINESS CHECKLIST:

- ☐ I'm open to whatever comes and know that I can't predict where this journey will take me.
- ☐ I'm willing to be vulnerable and share my experience with Rachel and the other members of the group.
- ☐ I'm willing to practice new skills and am committed to trying things I'm a beginner at.
- ☐ I'm open to the wisdom of my body.
- ☐ I acknowledge that diets have never served my happiness or health long-term.
- ☐ I'm willing to keep showing up even when I'm scared, frustrated, or having a hard time.
- ☐ I'm open to more happiness, ease, pleasure, trust and freedom in my life.
- ☐ I know that it's okay for me to ask for and make space in my life so as to give *Feast* the attention it and I deserve.
- ☐ I know that Rachel is committed to my success but, like me, is also an imperfect human being and will make mistakes. I know she is open to my constructive feedback and will do her best to support me however she can.

I know that if I get lost, behind or off track my reset buttons are:
- ☐ Placing a hand on my heart and taking several deep breaths.
- ☐ Reaching out to my buddy (if you have one).
- ☐ Reaching out to Rachel.
- ☐ Reaching out to the group on Facebook.
- ☐ Sharing my experience on the live calls.
- ☐ Asking myself: "What's most important for me right now on my learning journey?" and letting go of what isn't.
- ☐ Asking myself: "What's the kindest choice right now?"
- ☐ Starting again exactly where I am.
- ☐ Other:

My personal, human-sized intention for the next twelve weeks is:
_____.

Okay, are you ready?

I bet you are, but if there is anything from above that you haven't taken care of, make a note of it here and tackle it this week!

WEEK ONE

Self-Compassion

THE FOUNDATION

If you're like I was, you've read tons of books about "self-compassion" and get the idea intellectually, but struggle to put it into practice. Self-compassion is one of those phrases, like "authenticity" or "self-care" that can start to sound like Charlie Brown's teacher ("wah wah wah") when you hear it over and over again.

I invite you to come to this lesson without preconceived notions about what self-compassion is, so that you can truly understand why it is a fundamental practice for the well-fed woman.

THE FOSTER CHILD

I'm not a parent, or a foster parent, but I want you to imagine, however implausible, this scenario:

Your local child protective services agency arrives at your home with a young girl. She's young, six years old, and it's obvious that she's been through a lot during her short time on this earth. They explain that you are now entrusted with the care of this little girl. You are her parent.

While maybe you wouldn't have chosen to step into this role, you don't have a choice, so you decide that you're going to provide her with the most loving and stable home that you can. She deserves it.

The social worker warns you that she will try to test your love, and she does. She acts out and expects that you will abandon her, but you don't. You show her, as many times as it takes, that she can't push you away. With each tantrum she throws, or mean word she hurls your way, you pull her into your arms, brush the hair from her brow, and whisper loving words into her ear. You show her that your love for her isn't dependent on her being a certain way. You show her that that's not how love works.

Over time, you start to see the neural pathways in her very anxious nervous system begin to reroute themselves. Where she was once conditioned to be tight, tense, afraid, and uncertain of her caregivers, she is now relaxed, soft, and open. She knows you are not going anywhere. She knows your love is a constant. She knows, because you have shown her, that she is lovable just as she is.

I'm going to ask you to be a parent to the battered, scared, and wounded child at your doorstep, because she is you.

You may be worn down and weary, doubting that you're lovable, ashamed of yourself, or feeling incompetent and not enough. The weight of the world is on your shoulders. You need a mother, and that mother is within you.

MOTHERING

I'm going to guess that you're actual mother was not perfect. Mine certainly wasn't. She loved me, but she also judged me. I was lazy if I watched TV, vain if I cared about my style, selfish if I put my needs above others, and far too sensitive. My mother wasn't nearly affectionate enough. Growing up I felt a deep hunger for her touch, just to have her brush my hair or cuddle me. That just wasn't, isn't, my mother. She is wonderful in so many ways, but she wasn't able to provide all that I needed as a child.

But this isn't about my mother or yours.

This is about you and your ability to show up as a loving mother to yourself today. Accessing pure maternal love can be an excellent doorway for learning self-compassion.

If you can imagine that foster child needing you, and imagine expanding your heart to make room for her, then you can do the same for yourself.

You already know the basics of my journey from the welcome video, but I want to take you a bit deeper.

On September 13th, 2005 I moved from Washington, D.C. to the Bay Area, 3,000 miles away from anyone I knew. I was a perfectionist starting graduate school. I was an over stimulated highly sensitive person. I was a recovered anorexic about to slip into orthorexia (an obsession with "healthy eating") as a way to calm my newly stirred anxiety.

During my first three years in California, I lived in a three-bedroom apartment with a constantly changing cast of messy roommates. My bedroom was at the back of the house, dark and cramped by IKEA furniture that was too large for the space. Nevertheless, this compact and cave like room was my sanctuary from the world, and where I began to shine the light of compassion on my lonely, oh-so-tightly-wound, and hungry heart.

This didn't happen through some grand plan or how-to book, but out of moments quiet enough, and pain great enough, that a new voice began to emerge from within me.

I would take my lemon juice dressed lettuce, and boiled egg sprinkled with flax seeds up to my room, get under the covers, eat my insufficient dinner, and write in my journal.

This is what emerged:

"Dear Sweetheart, I'm sorry you're hurting."

"Dear Sweetheart, I'm here. I'm never leaving."

"Dear Sweetheart, tell me more. I want to hear it all."

Across pages and pages, over years and years, through tears and heartache, my inner mother wrote to me. I risked showing her my unedited gooey, secret insides. I confessed my most shameful bits, and she steadfastly reflected love back to me.

As she wrote, she loved me back until the veil of judgment lifted. Where I had once been so sure that I was unlovable, I now had proof that I was lovable because I loved myself.

In an interview with Oprah, the Buddhist monk, Thich Nhat Hanh, said of self-compassion:

> *"It's like a mother, when the baby is crying. She picks up the baby and she holds the baby tenderly in her arms. Your pain, your anxiety is your baby. You have to take care of it. You have to go back to yourself, to recognize the suffering in you, embrace the suffering and you get a relief."*

This is exactly what I did during those dark nights of my soul, and what I am inviting you to begin to do now.

It can't be emphasized enough how little this kind of mothering has to do with our own fallible mothers.

Pure inner maternal love is unshakable.

It's vaster than the eye can see, with an embrace so wide there's nothing that can't be cocooned within it.

It's patient and kind.

It's the softest place to fall, it doesn't judge, and it never wags a finger.

It's just love. And each of us (yes, you too) has the ability to tap into it, and shine its light on our inner weary, doubting, and malnourished child.

And yes, it takes time.

You are reconditioning your heart and rewiring parts of your brain.

That's okay. You've got time.

What lays in front of you is not a mountain to climb, though it might feel that way, but a quilt to patch together, stitch by stitch. Take a breath, thread your needle, sit back in the rocking chair, and slowly sew yourself whole.

Anytime you try to show yourself that you're not lovable ("See! I told you I'm _____"), or attempt to push yourself away, all you need to do is tap into your inner mamma self, into compassion, and into your commitment to reflect her love brightly back on you.

This is one giant, soul level trust fall.
This is where our *Feast* journey begins.

I'm asking you to be both the one who falls and the one who catches. And I'm asking you to let yourself fall again and again, and to catch yourself over and over.

THE NITTY GRITTY OF WHAT SELF-COMPASSION IS . . . AND ISN'T

Dr. Kristin Neff is the leading academic researcher on self-compassion (and she's this week's expert interviewee!). Because I think it's a good, comprehensive benchmark, I want to share with you the three-part definition of self-compassion from her website, *self-compassion.org*:

SELF KINDNESS

Self-compassion entails being warm and understanding toward ourselves when we suffer, fail, or feel inadequate, rather than ignoring our pain or flagellating ourselves with self-criticism. Self-compassionate people recognize that being imperfect, failing, and experiencing life difficulties is inevitable, so they tend to be gentle with themselves when confronted with painful experiences rather than getting angry when life falls short of set ideals. People cannot always be or get exactly what they want. When this reality is denied or fought against suffering increases in the form of stress, frustration and self-criticism. When this reality is accepted with sympathy and kindness, greater emotional equanimity is experienced.

COMMON HUMANITY

Frustration at not having things exactly as we want is often accompanied by an irrational but pervasive sense of isolation – as if "I" were the only person suffering or making mistakes. All humans suffer, however. The very definition of being "human" means that one is mortal, vulnerable and imperfect. Therefore, self-compassion involves recognizing that suffering and personal inadequacy is part of the shared human experience - something that we all go through rather than being something that happens to "me" alone.

MINDFULNESS

Self-compassion also requires taking a balanced approach to our negative emotions so that feelings are neither suppressed nor exaggerated. This…stems from the willingness to observe our negative thoughts and emotions with openness and clarity, so that they are held in mindful awareness. Mindfulness is a non-judgmental, receptive mind state in which one observes thoughts and feelings as they are, without trying to suppress or deny them. We cannot ignore our pain and feel compassion for it at the same time. At the same time, mindfulness requires that we not be "over-identified" with thoughts and feelings, so that we are caught up and swept away by negative reactivity.

WHAT SELF-COMPASSION IS NOT:

Self-compassion is not self-pity.

Self-pity arises when we feel separate from the rest of humanity, and like our pain is somehow different or greater than other people's pain ("Why does this always happen to *me*?"). Self-compassion holds our very valid experience in the larger awareness of our shared messy, imperfect, and painful human experience. When we practice self-compassion, rather than self-pity, we actually increase our ability to empathize and connect with other people.

Self-compassion is not a get-out-of-jail-free card.

Many of us believe that without a harsh inner voice, we would be lazy, a mess, and out of control. We believe that an inner whip cracking is essential to keep ourselves in line. Having self-compassion doesn't make us irresponsible; it empowers us to be more responsible for our feelings.

Geneen Roth, author of *Women, Food and God*, brilliantly wrote:

> *"For some reason, we are truly convinced that if we criticize ourselves, the criticism will lead to change. If we are harsh, we believe we will end up being kind. If we shame ourselves, we believe we end up loving ourselves. It has never been true, not for a moment, that shame leads to love. Only love leads to love."*

It's a tired, puritanical myth that if we no longer judge ourselves, we would eat bonbons all day, never lift a finger, and harm each other for personal gain. Self-compassion is an essential tool that lifts the misguiding haze of "good vs. bad" and returns us to a place where we can make choices.

To have self-compassion means treating ourselves with kindness, while being mindful of our individual and shared human experience. What happens from there is powerful enough to revolutionize anyone's life, but especially the lives of hungry women.

THE COMPASSIONATE ROAD AHEAD

When you begin to practice self-compassion, it might feel totally natural, or fake and forced. If you fall into the latter category, my suggestion is to practice anyway.

This is one of those times when "fake it till you make it" is good advice. After years of judging ourselves, our hearts can become a bit hardened. It takes time to thaw them.

Have compassion for the process.

Be as patient as you can, and continue to practice speaking compassionately to yourself when you have the awareness to do so. If this feels challenging, I recommend keeping a journal, like I did, where you can write to yourself from this new, more compassionate place.

In the end, self-compassion is: Practice, soften, and repeat. Practice, soften, and repeat.

Self-compassion is especially essential on our journey to becoming well-fed women. It allows us to drop our defenses and our need to run away, or numb out.

Think about it. If on the other side of your bedroom door was a cruel dictator, you wouldn't come out. But if on the other side of the door was a kind friend ready to serve you a delicious breakfast and listen to everything on your mind, you'd happily open the door. Self-compassion is about creating a safe, warm place for your whole self to come out.

When we, especially our scared and ashamed parts, know that we'll be met with self-compassion, welcoming our whole selves is instantly a safer and more appealing option. When we accept our whole selves, we have the opportunity to come into contact with our true hungers and our deepest wisdom. This is where choice lives, and making choices empowers us.

Too often, I see women approaching self-compassion like it is something to "work on," and add to their to do list. It triggers a, "I'll get to it when I have time," attitude that actually creates a distance between them and their self-compassion.

So, drop in and practice right now. Yes, right now. There's no better time. All it requires is an intention, presence, and softening.

You can practice self-compassion while you wash the dishes, drive to work, or balance your checkbook. There's no time when we can't look at our lives through this lens.

If at any point you feel lost, off track, or like you've taken a few steps backwards, THIS IS WHERE THE RESET BUTTON LIVES. All you need to do is turn towards yourself, messy life and all, and extend an embrace of love, acceptance, and validation.

This is the first step on the *Feast* journey. May we walk it with kindness.

WEEK ONE

REFLECTIONS ON SELF-COMPASSION

Describe your inner critic. What tone does it use? Does it sound like one of your parents? What are it's most common phrases or statements? What circumstances incite your inner critic? What circumstances calm your inner critic?

If your inner critic were in a crowd of a thousand inner critics how would you pick yours out? What are it's telltale traits?

What do you see as the impact your inner critic has on your life? What would be different if you inner critic were quieter or less powerful? What might be possible for your life if you were kinder and more compassionate toward yourself?

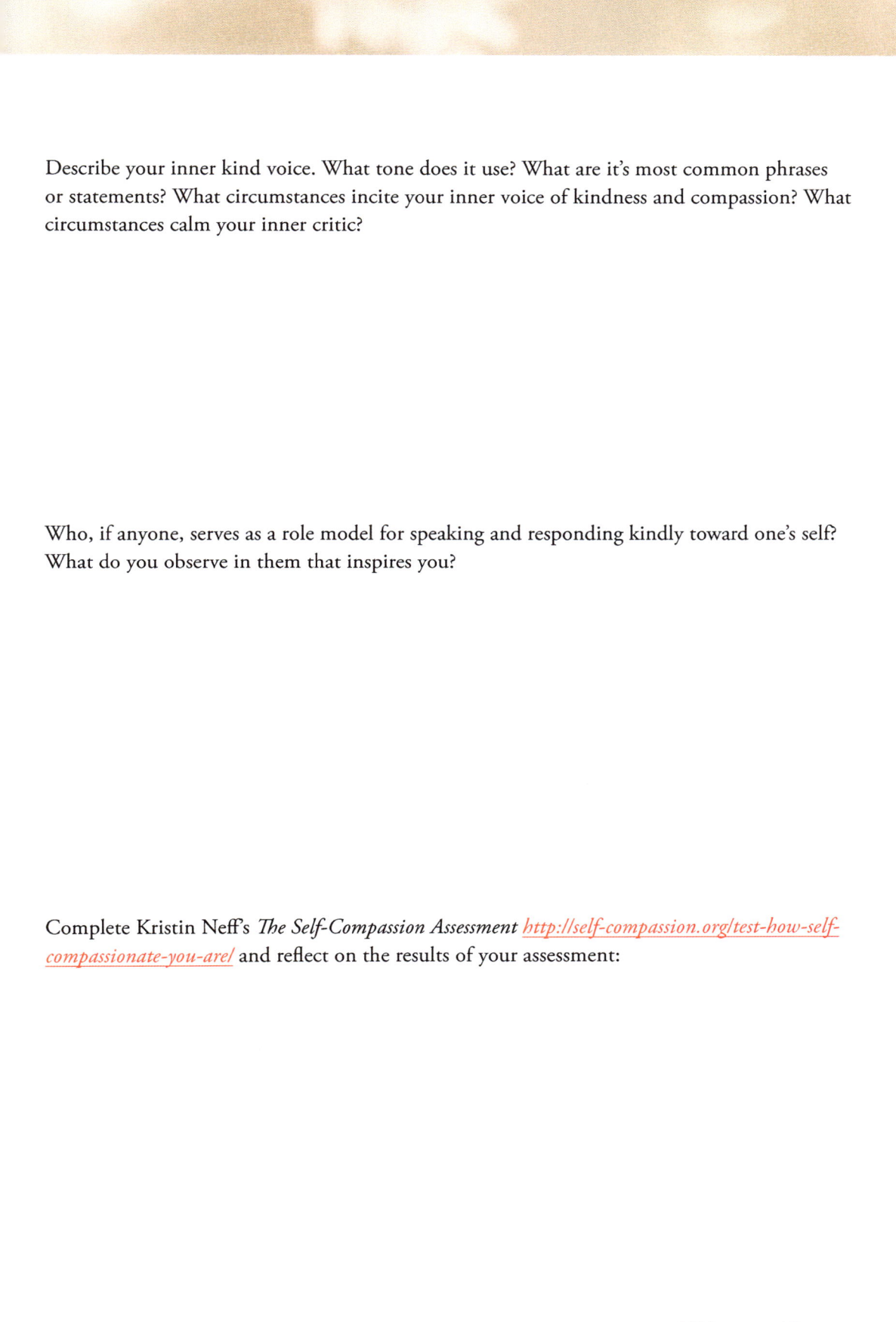

Describe your inner kind voice. What tone does it use? What are it's most common phrases or statements? What circumstances incite your inner voice of kindness and compassion? What circumstances calm your inner critic?

Who, if anyone, serves as a role model for speaking and responding kindly toward one's self? What do you observe in them that inspires you?

Complete Kristin Neff's *The Self-Compassion Assessment* http://self-compassion.org/test-how-self-compassionate-you-are/ and reflect on the results of your assessment:

WEEK ONE

SELF-COMPASSION CHALLENGE

For at least one full day, observe your judgmental and critical thought patterns. Record them using this chart. Note what event spurred the thought, what the thought was, what impact the thought had, and lastly, what a non-judgemental and compassionate thought might have been.

TRIGGER (event, thought, etc.)	JUDGEMENTAL THOUGHT	RESULT/IMPACT/ OUTCOME	SELF-COMPASSIONATE REFRAME
You had made plans with a friend, forgot, and stood her up.	"Ugh, I'm such a mess. I'm so self-absorbed that I'm a terrible friend. Why can't I get my life together?!"	Shame. Curt tone with everyone you encounter the rest of the day. "Fuck-it" binge eating later that night.	"I'm human. Everyone forgets things. Wow I can feel sadness for my friend, that she was stood up and sadness for me that I didn't get to see her. It feels icky to disappointment someone and I can be super tender with myself right now."

Now, practice speaking to and receiving yourself with compassion and kindness. One if the best ways to do this is to imagine how you might speak to and treat your daughter (real or imagined). You will practice this like you would if you were learning a new instrument. Frequently and with the understand that you won't be a prodigy right out the gate.

INSPIRING WORDS FOR PRACTICING SELF-COMPASSION

"It's like a mother, when the baby is crying, she picks up the baby and she holds the baby tenderly in her arms. Your pain, your anxiety is your baby. You have to take care of it. You have to go back to yourself, to recognize the suffering in you, embrace the suffering, and you get a relief."

THICH NHAT HANH

"Self-compassion is approaching ourselves, our inner experience with spaciousness, with the quality of allowing which has a quality of gentleness. Instead of our usual tendency to want to get over something, to fix it, to make it go away, the path of compassion is totally different. Compassion allows."

ROBERT GONZALES

"Compassion isn't some kind of self-improvement project or ideal that we're trying to live up to. Having compassion starts and ends with having compassion for all those unwanted parts of ourselves, all those imperfections that we don't even want to look at."

PEMA CHODRON

"For some reason, we are truly convinced that if we criticize ourselves, the criticism will lead to change. If we are harsh, we believe we will end up being kind. If we shame ourselves, we believe we end up loving ourselves. It has never been true, not for a moment, that shame leads to love. Only love leads to love."

GENEEN ROTH

WEEK ONE

EXPERT INTERVIEWEE

Kristin Neff

Kristin studied communications as an undergraduate at the University of California at Los Angeles (B.A., 1988). She did her graduate work at University of California at Berkeley (Ph.D., 1997), studying moral development with Dr. Elliot Turiel. Her dissertation research was conducted in Mysore, India, where she examined children's moral reasoning. She then spent two years of post-doctoral study with Dr. Susan Harter at Denver University, studying issues of authenticity and self-concept development. Her current position at the University of Texas at Austin started in 1999, and she was promoted to Associate Professor in 2006.

During Kristin's last year of graduate school in 1997 she became interested in Buddhism, and has been practicing meditation in the Insight Meditation tradition ever since. While doing her post-doctoral work she decided to conduct research on self-compassion – a central construct in Buddhist psychology and one that had not yet been examined empirically.

In addition to her pioneering research into self-compassion, she has developed an 8-week program to teach self-compassion skills. The program, co-created with her colleague Chris Germer, affiliated with Harvard Medical School, is called Mindful Self-Compassion. Her book, Self-Compassion, was published by William Morrow in April, 2011. To learn more about Kristin and her work visit *self-compassion.org*.

NOTES

Want more?

Then check out these related posts that Rachel has written.

TERMS OF ENDEARMENT
goo.gl/lHYzdR

THE FOOLPROOF WAY TO KNOW YOU ARE LOVABLE
goo.gl/mtlkwo

SELF-COMPASSION IS A VERB
goo.gl/onwaHv

CRAWL INTO YOUR OWN LAP
goo.gl/Lm6YO3

WEEK ONE

NOTES

NOTES

WEEK ONE

GENERAL *FEAST* SKILLS	S 7/31	M 8/1	T 8/2	W 8/3	Th 8/4	F 8/5	Sa 8/6
Meditated (on own or with recording)							
Read Feast Material							
Wrote responses to reflection questions							
Listened to expert interview/live call							
Reached out to the group for support							
Meditated (on own or with recording)							
Meditated (on own or with recording)							

SELF-COMPASSION SKILLS	S 7/31	M 8/1	T 8/2	W 8/3	Th 8/4	F 8/5	Sa 8/6
Spoke kindly to myself							
Acted self-compassionately toward myself							

WEEK TWO

Caring for Your Sensitive Soul

THE FOUNDATION

GROWING UP AS A MEMORY FOAM MATTRESS

The best way to describe how I felt as a child is like an intuitive (psychic, even), memory foam mattress. I could feel the inner emotional landscape of anyone around me. Other people's feelings left me with a deep, slow-to-release indentation.

It always seemed like my interactions with the world, large and small, had a bigger impact on me than on my family members. Put another way, life felt like a paper towel commercial, and I was always the super absorbent one.

Yes, I am a Highly Sensitive Person.

In the early days of elementary school, I was known for walking my fellow classmates, who I thought needed someone to talk to, down to the school counselor's office. I did this unprompted by an adult. No joke.

Certain physical sensations were intolerable to me: the texture of dryer lint, the feeling of sleeping under a tucked in top sheet, the grittiness of sugar crystals on a cookie against my teeth.

At a parent-teacher conference, my teacher told my parents that sometimes, rather than play with other children, I would sincerely ask my teacher how her marriage was going.

I felt more deeply and empathized more effortlessly with the world than other children.

My parents might as well have given birth to an alien given how different I was from them, and from my much less emotional sister. I was told, "You're too sensitive," more times than I can count.

The feedback from my family, both subtle and explicit, was that I was high maintenance, a burden at times, and wrong in how I reacted to the world around me. How they responded to me was an easy recipe for my feeling ashamed.

What they didn't know, and more importantly, what I didn't know, was that there was an explanation for why I was this way. I say explanation and not diagnosis because there was, and is, nothing wrong me.

I am a Highly Sensitive Person (HSP).

Does what I'm describing sound familiar? If so, you might be one too. If you're not, you certainly know one. According to Dr. Elaine Aron, author of The Highly Sensitive Person, we make up 15-20 percent of the population.

Not only is there nothing wrong with me or my fellow HSPs, but having this temperament can be a huge asset once we know how to care for our sensitive souls.

WHAT IT MEANS TO BE AN HSP

Carl Jung originally coined the term "innate sensitiveness." In the 1990's, Aron pioneered the entire HSP field of study. She dove deep into what it means for a person to have high sensory processing sensitivity, and identified four common traits of HSPs:

- DEPTH OF PROCESSING: HSPs constantly need to pause, check in with themselves, and process what is happening before they can move forward.

- OVER AROUSAL: What non-HSPs find mildly arousing is highly arousing for HSPs (e.g. the temperature or lighting in a room). When HSPs are over aroused (e.g. physically alert, awake, experiencing an increased heart rate) they often need to withdraw or shut down.

- EMOTIONAL REACTIVITY AND HIGH EMPATHY: HSPs have stronger emotions, feel more deeply, and are better able to understand and share in how others feel.

- SENSITIVITY TO SUBTLE STIMULI: Stimulation comes from a myriad of sources, including our five senses and our energetic body. HSPs are more astute at perceiving understated stimuli. One or more of their senses may be heightened as compared to non-HSPs. Some HSPs may even identify as having a "sixth sense."

Take a moment to reflect on what senses contribute to your feeling over stimulated:

SIGHT	Bright and fluorescent lights Busy urban scene Visually stimulating museum exhibit Intense movie or theater performance
SMELL	Intense aroma (e.g. perfume store) Specific irritating scent (e.g. sulfur)
SOUND	Loud music Certain types of music (e.g. heavy metal) Repetitive sounds (e.g. ticking clock)
TASTE	Spicy food Hot or cold food Highly seasoned foods
TOUCH	Itchy fabrics Hot or cold weather Tight clothing Sexual intimacy Children's need for physical contact
ENERGETIC AND EMOTIONAL BODY	Mood in a room People with a 'bad' or 'sad' vibe Restaurant with an 'off' atmosphere Being in a caregiving role Co-dependent relationships Excessive screen time

THREE MYTHS ABOUT BEING AN HSP

1. HSPS ARE WEAK AND FRAGILE

As the author of Divine Living, Anthon St. Maarten, wrote, "Highly sensitive people are too often perceived as weaklings or damaged goods. To feel intensely is not a symptom of weakness, it is the trademark of the truly alive and compassionate."

While HSPs do have different care requirements than non-HSPs, and feel more easily and deeply than non-HSPS, they are also often more resilient, and possess certain increased intelligences.

2. HSPS ARE HIGH-MAINTENANCE AND A BURDEN

It's important to differentiate between high maintenance and differently maintained. HSPs have a different "user manual" than non-HSPs. Because we live in a world dominated by non-HSPs, HSPs' needs can be incorrectly perceived as excessive. Once we understand and celebrate that all people have different needs, strengths, and challenges, we can better provide for this diversity. It is especially important for HSPs to understand their own needs so that they can take the lead in their care and communicate their needs to others.

3. ALL HSPS ARE INTROVERTS AND ALL HSPS ARE THE SAME

Many HSPs are introverted, but not all of them. According to Aron, 30% are extroverts. HSPs are incredibly diverse and exist across a spectrum of sensitivity. If you identify with some of the HSP traits, but not all of them, it doesn't mean you aren't an HSP, it means you are one kind of an HSP.

BEING AN HSP AND A WELL-FED WOMAN

As a sensitive child, it's no surprise that I grew into a sensitive adult.

It wasn't until I was in my late twenties that I first heard the term Highly Sensitive Person. Up until then, I had no idea that so much of my experience could be explained by understanding my temperament. Learning about HSPs felt like finding a missing piece of myself. Perhaps as you read this, you're also feeling puzzle pieces click into place.

HSPs have different care requirements than non-HSPs, and each HSP has her own care requirements that may be different from other HSPs. Not knowing this, I spent years trying to make myself behave like a non-HSP, and felt guilty when seemingly simple, normal activities would over stimulate me.

The sensation I've learned to become keenly aware of is of being "overloaded," or feeling like my nervous system is shutting down. The more stimulation I experience, the more my circuits want to go dark, and I need to withdraw, and retreat to safety.

For example, after a weekend that includes several social engagements, my body will say, "Let's stay in bed today, and maybe tomorrow too, to restore ourselves." Or when I'm in a very loud, crowded space I'll hear my body whisper, "Let's go find some place quieter." I experience overload in weather that my body finds too hot, cold, dry, or damp; in places with bright, fluorescent lights; and when I use cleaning or bath products that are too harsh for my skin. I can also become overloaded from the depth of my feelings.

Up through my late twenties, one of the ways I calmed myself was through food. While this worked in the moment, it wasn't effective in the long run because it left me physically unwell.

I traded overstimulation for a painful, bloated stomach. As I came to own being an HSP, and began living in my body, I became highly attuned to my capacity for stimulation and to what calmed my nervous system.

This second foundational week is dedicated to the topic of caring for the sensitive soul because: a. sensitive women are often drawn to this course, b. many of us carry unnecessary shame and judgment about our sensitive nature, and/or don't understand how to live as an HSP, and c. chaotic eating can often be mitigated by proper care and tending to our sensitive souls.

There are three challenges I see when it comes to HSPs' relationship with food:

1. You don't know that you are an HSP, so you live your life expecting to be able to operate like a non-HSP, which results in overstimulation and intense emotions that you soothe through food.

2. You know you are an HSP, but aren't aware of the internal cues that signal when you are moderately or overly stimulated. Your connection to your own HSP gauge isn't up and running yet, so when you become over stimulated, you soothe yourself with food.

3. You know you are an HSP, and that overstimulation can lead to self-soothing through eating, but you don't know how else to calm your nervous system.

If you identify with the first challenge, hopefully by the end of this week's lesson, you'll know whether, or not you are an HSP.

Overcoming the second challenge requires that you tune your body to learn when your HSP gauge is creeping up towards "highly stimulated."

Consciously practicing new self-soothing activities when you find yourself defaulting to food will help you transform the third challenge. Self-soothing with food is not "bad," but you want to have more than one tool in your toolbox, as well as tools that leave you feeling better rather than worse.

Other ways that HSPs struggle with food include:

- When HSPs are over stimulated, or near burnout, it's difficult for them to know what they are hungry for and when they've had enough to eat.

- A stimulating environment (e.g. a crowded, loud restaurant) make it challenging for HSPs to stay connected to what their food tastes like, and their body's hunger and fullness signals.

- Rather than overeat, some HSPs self-soothe by not eating or weighing themselves frequently. Both eating and not eating to calm our nervous systems can lead to us away from ourselves and from feeling our best.

CARING FOR YOUR SENSITIVE SOUL

You'll have this whole week to sink into how being a sensitive person has impacted your life. To start, here are five ways to care for your sensitive soul:

- **FORGIVE YOURSELF.**
  If you've been harsh toward your sensitive temperament, let it go and embrace it with gentleness. If you've used food as a way to cope with being an HSP, have compassion for the part of you that did its best to take care of you however it could.

- **EMBRACE YOUR TEMPERAMENT'S STRENGTHS AND CHALLENGES.** To the extent that you can, accept the whole you. You are human after all.

- **OBSERVE YOURSELF.**
  Become curious about your unique sensitivities. Become an expert in you.

- **CREATE YOUR OWN "CARE MANUAL."**
  What do you and important people in your life need to know about your unique care needs?

- **NOTICE WHICH OF YOUR SENSES IS ASKING FOR CALM.**
  Overstimulation comes through our senses, so it's our senses that often need soothing. Which of your senses needs soothing this week?

WEEK TWO

REFLECTIONS FOR THE SENSITIVE SOUL

To start, complete *Elaine Aron's HSP Assessment* *www.hsperson.com/test/highly-sensitive-test*

Were you ever told that you were too sensitive? Who told you this? How did it make you feel?

What are you sensitive to? (i.e. music, noise, people, crowds, other's energy, light, smells, tastes, clutter, chaos, traffic, roller coasters, temperature, touch, other's pain/joy, etc.)

Reflect on your day-to-day life. What sensory inputs do you regularly encounter? Which do you find yourself easily overloaded with?

How does being sensitive relate to your relationship with food? Do you turn to food when you are overstimulated?

How do you, or might you, care for yourself given the sensitivities you identified here? What are a few specific strategies you might employ?

Identify an instance where your heightened sensitivity has served you (and others). What has been the gift in this temperament?

WEEK TWO

CHALLENGES FOR THE SENSITIVE SOUL

Make one small adjustment in your environment or relationships to make them more supportive of your sensitivities.

Tell someone in your life about your sensitivities in a non-apologetic way. Simply educate them about your temperament and inform them as to what they can do to support you. You might say, for example, "Hey. So I'm learning about this thing called HSP. It stands for Highly Sensitive Person and it's predisposed temperament/personality trait that affects 15-20% of the population. Turns out it fits me to a tee/It's like my whole life makes sense now, and I'm learning that what works best for me is/what I need is/___doesn't work for me. I wanted to let you know so that we can both enjoy the best version of me."

If it's helpful, practice using a 1 to 10 scale for checking in with yourself on your level of stimulation. Notice where you are on the scale when you start to feel overstimulated and what internal or external symptoms tell you this is happening.

EXPERT INTERVIEWEE

Kate Read

Kate Read received her Bachelor of Arts Degree in Psychology from Fairfield University in the spring of 2006. She went on to receive her holistic nutrition training and certification at the Institute for Integrative Nutrition ® earning accreditation from The American Association of Drugless Practitioners (AADP) and Purchase College, SUNY. Before founding Kate Read, LLC in January of 2011, Kate worked in digital advertising media in New York City.

Inspired by Ane Axford's Sensitive Leadership Program which utilizes The Highly Sensitive Hierarchy of Needs™ (HSHN), Kate completed Ane's 10-month course in order to enhance her ability to serve this (often neglected) sensitive niche. Kate later ventured down the path of energy healing, getting her Level II Reiki Certification (Usui Reiki Ryoho) while working closely with a private healing center in NYC. She is in the process of earning a Universal Health Principals certification which combines scientific knowledge of the universe coupled with direct conversation with the body and it's biofield.

Kate currently lives in the green mountains of Waterbury Vermont where she remotely runs her 1:1 coaching practice full-time. She is heavily involved in the healing arts community at the Vermont Center for Integrative Therapy, and continues to participate in programs that help her to better serve her own well being as well as her growing sensitive following. To learn more about Kate and her work visit *homeforthehighlysensitive.com*.

WEEK TWO

NOTES

NOTES

WEEK TWO

DAILY PRACTICE CHECKLIST

GENERAL *FEAST* SKILLS	S 8/7	M 8/8	T 8/9	W 8/10	Th 8/11	F 8/12	Sa 8/13
Meditated (on own or with recording)							
Read Feast Material							
Wrote responses to reflection questions							
Listened to expert interview/live call							
Reached out to the group for support							
Meditated (on own or with recording)							
Meditated (on own or with recording)							

SELF-COMPASSION SKILLS	S 8/7	M 8/8	T 8/9	W 8/10	Th 8/11	F 8/12	Sa 8/13
Spoke kindly to myself							
Acted self-compassionately toward myself							

CARE FOR SENSITIVE SOUL SKILLS	S 8/7	M 8/8	T 8/9	W 8/10	Th 8/11	F 8/12	Sa 8/13
Attempted to mangage my sensory input							
Advocated for my HSP needs							
Celebrated/observed my HSP strengths							

WEEK THREE

Effective Emotional Coping

THE FOUNDATION

I lived out a cliché as a child: I was certain there was a monster in my closet.

My mother would try to calm my nerves by turning on the light, looking in the closet, and quietly telling me, "Rachel, there's no monster in your closet." And she was right, there wasn't, but every night I was still afraid.

As adults, when it comes to uncomfortable emotions, we often feel like if we really experience them, all hell will break loose. They'll take over our life and last forever. Uncomfortable emotions are our monsters. This week, you're going to turn the light on in your closet, so that you can see that the feelings you've been avoiding aren't as terrifying as your mind is telling you they are.

I'm always surprised by the lengths humans will go to, myself included, in order to avoid uncomfortable emotions. We'll stay in a bad relationship to avoid feeling guilt for breaking someone's heart. We'll ask for less from life to avoid disappointment. We'll go into debt to avoid feeling scarcity.

And yes, we'll eat ourselves sick to avoid even the most basic of emotional discomforts. Uncomfortable feelings can be so intolerable that avoiding them can seem like the only option.

Two things cause this discomfort, my loves: 1. The four myths about emotions, and 2. Not having effective, non-harming coping mechanisms. This week, we'll address both of these causes. Today: the myths. Later this week: some awesome new tools!

When we unmask the myths and use these tools, you'll no longer need to run away from the monsters in your mind. Monsters, who, once the light is turned on, will turn out to be allies with valuable information for you.

MYTHS ABOUT EMOTIONS

I truly used to believe that my anxiety, fear, sadness, anger, and shame would kill me if I stopped eating, or exercising, and actually felt them. This and other myths kept me trapped. Which of the myths below has trapped you?

MYTH 1: I CAN'T HANDLE THIS FEELING

Heartbreak, anxiety, rage, fear and other strong emotions can feel so uncomfortable and threatening that our brain will react as if we're covered from head to toe in killer bees. The message is, "Get the hell away from this feeling as soon as possible before it kills you." In reality, we're totally safe and free from impending doom.

Joe Kowan, in his Ted Talk, "How I Beat Stage Fright," shared this brilliant observation:

> *"I mean, your nervous system is an idiot. Really? Two hundred thousand years of human evolution, and it still can't tell the difference between a saber-toothed tiger and 20 folk singers on a Tuesday night Open Mic?"*

When our survival instincts kick in, we often numb and distract ourselves through food, shopping, alcohol, television, Facebook, etc. without realizing that the feeling can't harm us. In fact, it might help us. Too often we, consciously or unconsciously, believe that we're not up for the task of feeling our uncomfortable feelings.

Here's the truth: Feelings will never kill us. They can't.

No one has ever died from feelings. They will not overtake you. They will not eat you alive. It's a fact.

MYTH 2: THIS FEELING WILL LAST FOREVER

Many of us believe that if we open the door, even a crack, to our feelings they will flood us like a dam breaking and we'll never be OK again. We think that dropping into our sadness, anxiety, or anger will take us into a bottomless pit of despair.

This too is not so.

Unfelt feelings calcify.

Felt feelings pass. They always pass.

One of my favorite passages from Women Food and God, by Geneen Roth, addresses this beautifully. Roth says:

"All any feeling wants is to be welcomed with tenderness. It wants room to unfold. It wants to relax and tell its story. It wants to dissolve like a thousand writhing snakes that with a flick of kindness become harmless strands of rope."

Feelings dissolve when we welcome them.

And as you'll discover in Thursday's expert interview, they can dissolve rather quickly.

> **Reminder!**
>
> This week please read Chapter Eleven in *Intuitive Eating*.

MYTH 3: MY FEELINGS ARE INCONVENIENT. THEY GET IN THE WAY OF WHAT I HAVE TO DO. I DON'T HAVE TIME TO STOP AND FEEL _____.

It's natural to believe that negative or painful experiences are detours or barriers to our life, but in fact, our life is made up of all of our experiences. All of life's events, whether they are easy or hard, joyful or full of anguish, are our path. They are not a detour.

Spiritual teacher and poet, Mark Nepo, put it so eloquently when he wrote in The Endless Practice, "The point of experience is not to escape life, but to live it."

As much as we only want to feel happiness, joy, and elation, we must also experience difficult emotions. We can't have one without the other. Together they create the rich tapestry that is human life. As Brené Brown explains in The Gifts of Imperfection, "We cannot selectively numb emotions, when we numb the painful emotions, we also numb the positive emotions."

Experiencing all of our feelings is our path, not an obstruction to our path. All of our feelings, easy and challenging, can serve as deep resources of wisdom. Listening to our pain can provide the answers and healing we have long been seeking.

MYTH 4: IF I FEEL IT, I'LL HAVE TO FIX IT.

If you feel it, you'll feel it.

Nothing more is required.

If you are ignoring some part of your life that is trying to get your attention (via a feeling) you can kick that can down the road a bit longer by numbing out, but chances are you're here because you are bone-tired of being numb. Am I right?

The voices inside us that reinforce these myths, don't have to go away, but they don't get to run the show anymore either. When you have the thought, "I can't handle this feeling," simply say hello to that thought, and make the choice to guide your thoughts in a different direction.

RESTORING CHOICE

The first step to managing our uncomfortable emotions is to restore choice to the places where we mindlessly veer away from feeling our feelings. For many of us, this avoidance takes the form of eating, but it can also look like drinking wine, binge-watching TV, or simply telling ourselves, "Buck up!"

None of these responses is inherently bad, or even a problem, but for many of us they don't feel like choices. They feel like involuntary reflexes (like a doctor tapping on our knee).

THE MOST IMPORTANT STEP IN MANAGING OUR UNCOMFORTABLE EMOTIONS IS TO RESTORE CHOICE.

When we pause between having a feeling and acting to suppress it, we become powerful.

Repeat after me: "Pausing to make a choice is everything."

The pause is a fork in the road. Whether you go left or right is far less important than that you make a choice.

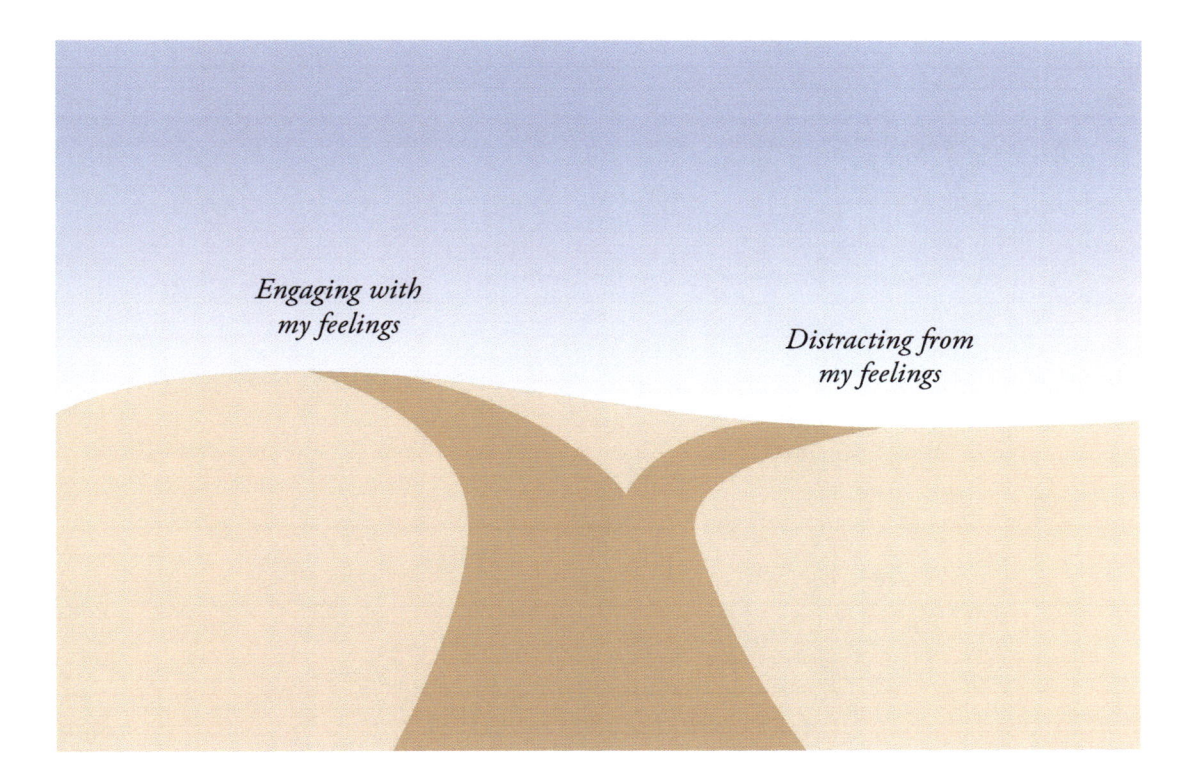

Engaging with my feelings

Distracting from my feelings

So what are the two paths?

Path one is to engage with the feeling. You choose to feel what you are feeling.

Path two is to distract yourself from the feeling. You choose not to feel your feelings.

Neither of these paths is better than the other, but we want to grow our capacity to take the first path because it supports our being more choiceful and limber. It helps us to become empowered. Sometimes, the first path doesn't feel possible in that moment. When that happens, *choosing* the second path is totally acceptable.

PRACTICE PAUSING

Later this week we'll dive deeper into specific practices for each of these practices. For now, I want you to practice pausing for ten seconds when you have an uncomfortable emotion. That's it, ten seconds, then go ahead and do whatever you want. Simply practice pausing.

If you are someone who doesn't always know how you feel, practice pausing for ten seconds throughout the day, or right before bed, and ask yourself:

- What is the best way I can describe my emotions right now?
- Without labeling my experience as good or bad, what emotions, thoughts and physical sensations do I observe?

That's it for today. Just practice pausing for 10 seconds.

WEEK THREE

REFLECTIONS ON COPING WITH EMOTIONS

Four of the most common myths about emotions are:
"I can't handle feeling this."
"It will last forever if I feel it."
"This feeling is getting in the way of my life."
"If I feel it, I'll have to fix it."

Do you find yourself operating under any of these myths? If so when/where do you see this showing up in your life? What's the impact of believing this/these myths?

GETTING TO KNOW YOUR EMOTIONS CHART
Source: DBT Made Simple (2013) by Sheri Van Dijk

EMOTION	BODY RESPONSE (physical sensations, body language, facial expressions)	THOUGHTS (including memories, images, and judgements)	URGES (what you feel like doing when feeling the emotion)	BEHAVIORS (what you actually do when feeling the emotion)	CONSEQUENCES (impact or effect of the behavior, such as self-judgement, stomach ache, poor sleep, missed work)
ANGER					
HAPPINESS					

WEEK THREE

EMOTION	BODY RESPONSE (physical sensations, body language, facial expressions)	THOUGHTS (including memories, images, and judgements)	URGES (what you feel like doing when feeling the emotion)	BEHAVIORS (what you actually do when feeling the emotion)	CONSEQUENCES (impact or effect of the behavior, such as self-judgement, stomach ache, poor sleep, missed work)
SADNESS					
FEAR					
LOVE					
SHAME/ GUILT					
Add any emotion here					
Add any emotion here					
Add any emotion here					

Once you've completed your chart reflect. What did you notice? Any surprises?

What do you know about how do you typically cope with discomfort, pain, and stress?

Reflect on the ways you currently cope in your life. Which ways are effective? and ineffective? What works in the short term but not the long-term? What works in the long-term, but is hard in the short term?

What messages did you get growing up about difficult or strong emotions? What role models did you have for experiencing intense emotions? What role models did you have for healthy or unhealthy coping skills?

WEEK THREE

INTUITIVE EATING QUESTIONS / CHAPTER ELEVEN

Your reading assignment this week is Chapter 11 in *Intuitive Eating*. On page 151 the authors outline the continuum of emotional eating. Do you see your behaviors in this continuum? If so where?

In Chapter 11, which line or passage was the most powerful? Transcribe here:

Did this week's reading assignment leave you with any questions?

Review this chart of emotions and see if there are any emotions you have difficulty staying with or a maybe-not-true preexisting belief about:

PRIMARY EMOTION	SECONDARY EMOTION	TERTIARY EMOTIONS
LOVE	AFFECTION	Adoration, affection, love, fondness, liking, attraction, caring, tenderness, compassion, sentimentality
LOVE	LUST	Arousal, desire, lust, passion, infatuation
LOVE	LONGING	Longing
JOY	CHEERFUL	Amusement, bliss, cheerfulness, gaiety, glee, jolliness, joviality, joy, delight, enjoyment, gladness, happiness, jubilation, elation, satisfaction, ecstasy, euphoria
JOY	ZEST	Enthusiasm, zeal, zest, excitement, thrill, exhilaration
JOY	CONTENTMENT	Contentment, pleasure
JOY	PRIDE	Pride, triumph
JOY	OPTIMISM	Eagerness, hope, optimism
JOY	ENTHRALLMENT	Enthrallment, rapture
JOY	RELIEF	Relief
SURPRISE	SURPRISE	Amazement, surprise, astonishment

WEEK THREE

PRIMARY EMOTION	SECONDARY EMOTION	TERTIARY EMOTIONS
ANGER	IRRITATION	Aggravation, irritation, agitation, annoyance, grouchiness, grumpiness
	EXASPERATION	Exasperation, frustration
	RAGE	Anger, rage, outrage, fury, wrath, hostility, ferocity, bitterness, hate, loathing, scorn, spite, vengefulness, dislike, resentment
	DISGUST	Disgust, revulsion, contempt
	ENVY, JEALOUSY	Torment
	TORMENT	Torment
SADNESS	SUFFERING	Agony, suffering, hurt, anguish
	SADNESS	Depression, despair, hopelessness, gloom, glumness, sadness, unhappiness, grief, sorrow, woe, misery, melancholy
	DISAPPOINTMENT	Dismay, disappointment, displeasure
	SHAME	Guilt, shame, regret, remorse
	NEGLECT	Alienation, isolation, neglect, loneliness, rejection, homesickness, defeat, dejection, insecurity, embarrassment, humiliation, insult
	SYMPATHY	Pity, sympathy
FEAR	HORROR	Alarm, shock, fear, fright, horror, terror, panic, hysteria, mortification
	NERVOUSNESS	Anxiety, nervousness, tenseness, uneasiness, apprehension, worry, distress, dread

Source: Shaver, P., Schwartz, J., Kirson, D., & O'Connor, C. (2001). *Emotional Knowledge: Further Exploration of a Prototype Approach. In G. Parrott (Eds.), Emotions in Social Psychology: Essential Readings* (pp. 26-56). Philadelphia, PA: Psychology Press.

CHALLENGES FOR EFFECTIVE EMOTIONAL COPING

As you know by now, your primary task when it comes to coping with difficult emotions is to find a moment to pause. This moment occurs when you're feeling a strong or challenging emotion and instead of unconsciously barreling ahead toward distraction, numbing, or checking out you're able to find just one moment (even 5 or 10 seconds) where you can pause and make a choice about how you want to proceed.

Once you find the pause button you get to choose between turning left, toward engaging, or right, toward distracting, neither of which is necessarily superior to the other, we simply want you to feel choiceful.

Yes, it's true that we want you to feel capable of feeling your emotions not least of which is because a felt emotion is an emotion that passes. A felt emotion is also an emotion that decreases in intensity which gives us less need to self-soothe. That said, there are times when the best choice or the only choice is to distract, at least for a time, and this is perfectly wise self-care.

Today and over the weekend practice a new coping skill from the lists below. If this feels daunting simply try the new coping tool for 2-5 minutes. Remember to stay with it using your non-judgemental observer mind as much as possible.

COPING SKILLS FOR WHEN YOU WANT TO OR FEEL UP FOR ENGAGING WITH THE FEELINGS

1. URGE SURFING

The fact is that urges don't last long, almost never more than half an hour if not fulfilled. Few people give themselves the opportunity to witness this phenomenon.

To practice urge surfing, set a timer for dedicated amount of time (10 or 15 minutes is good) and simply sit comfortably. Note the sensation of your breath going in and out. Notice any sensations of the urge. Note any thoughts that arise ("Ugh, I really just want to go eat the whole gallon of ice cream so I don't have to feel how stressed out I am!"). Let any thoughts drift by like clouds in a sky. Notice any shifts in how the urge is feeling in your body. Notice if the intensity of the urge shifts. As you're noticing bring your awareness to the sensation of your breath as it moves in and out. Keep observing, feeling, and allowing. If when the timer goes off you still want to go do the behavior, go do it. If you feel the urge has lessened or you have

WEEK THREE

some space between it to make a different choice, then honor that.

2. RAIN

I learned this practice from Tara Brach. Here are a few of her guidepoints:

STEP 1: RECOGNIZE WHAT IS GOING ON.

"Recognizing means consciously acknowledging, in any given moment, the thoughts, feelings, and behaviors that are affecting us."

STEP 2: ALLOW YOUR EXPERIENCE TO BE JUST AS IT IS

"Allowing means letting the thoughts, emotions, feelings, or sensations we have recognized simply be there…We allow by simply pausing with the intention to relax our resistance and let the experience be just as it is."

STEP 3: INVESTIGATE WITH KINDNESS

"Investigating means calling on our natural curiosity—the desire to know truth—and directing a more focused attention to our present experience. Simply pausing to ask, what is happening inside me?, can initiate recognition, but investigation adds a more active and pointed kind of inquiry. What am I believing? What does this feeling want from me? You might notice hollowness or shakiness, then discover a sense of unworthiness and shame masked by those feelings. Unless you bring them into awareness, your unconscious beliefs and emotions will control your experience and perpetuate your identification with a limited, deficient self."

STEP 4: NATURAL AWARENESS (RATHER THAN IDENTIFYING WITH THE EXPERIENCE)

"Natural loving awareness occurs when identification with the small self is loosened. This practice of non-identification means that our sense of who we are is not fused with any limiting emotions, sensations, or stories. We begin to intuit and live from the openness and love that express our natural awareness…There's nothing to do for this last part of RAIN; we simply rest in natural awareness."

Source: http://www.mindful.org/mindful-magazine/tara-brach-rain-mindfulness-practice

3. JOURNALING WITH COMPASSION.

Pretty self explanatory. Write it out. Tell the truth. Don't edit yourself or hold back. Don't try to write well. Just write it out, including all of your feelings, and meet your experience with the soft heart of compassion. You can use a prompt, such as: "The truth of the matter is…" or "My heart would say…"

4. COST-BENEFIT ANALYSIS

This skill is useful when you feel an urge to go behave in a way that isn't generally helpful. For example, if you're upset you might feel the urge to step on the scale and weigh yourself, even though you know that doing this wouldn't help and could be very triggering. Start by making four lists, (1) the benefits of the destructive coping behavior, (2) the cost of the destructive coping behavior, (3) the benefits of the supportive coping behavior, and (4) the costs of the supportive coping behavior. Now give each item on each list a weight or value from 1-5. 1 = very little importance and 5 = high importance. Once you've assigned values add the benefits of the destructive behavior with the costs of the healthy behavior. Then add the costs of the destructive behavior with the benefits of the healthy behavior. See which one results in a bigger numerical (and benefit) value.

Source: Van Dijk, S. (2009) The Dialectical Behavior Therapy Skills Workbook for Bipolar Disorder: Using DBT to Regain Control of Your Emotions and Your Life. New Harbinger Publications.

5. REFRAME

This is when we make lemonade out of lemons. It's not always available to us in distressing moments, but when we can take a step back at a situation and reframe it positively our negative emotions tend to decline in intensity. To practice, ask yourself "How else could I look at this?" or "Is there a silver lining here?" Another way to approach reframing is to write down the version of the story that you're telling yourself and the version of the story that is closer to the factual truth.

6. GO IN SLO-MO

Don't change your behavior or the trajectory of your actions, just do everything in s l o - m o. Pretend you're at half speed. Walk slow. Eat slow. Lift things slowly. See what happens when you slow everything down and create space to non-judgmentally observe.

WEEK THREE

COPING SKILLS FOR WHEN YOU WANT TO DISTRACT FROM THE FEELINGS (AND MAKE A CONSCIOUS CHOICE TO DO SO)

First say, without any judgement and with a lot of compassion, to yourself "I'm choosing to distract from what I'm feeling right now. This is me taking care of myself the best way I can in this moment." Second, really allow yourself be distracted.

Here is a list of non-harming activities that help to distract:

- *Find your funny (watch a funny television show, listen to a stand up comic, read a funny book.)*
- *Clean, organize, or groom (mop the floors, put all your shoes in colored order, trim your cuticles.)*
- *Do something with your hands (knit, doodle, play with silly putty, sew on a missing button)*
- *Play a game (crossword, solitaire, words with friends)*
- *Reach out (ask a friend to hang out or go to the movies)*
- *Take a nap or go to bed early.*
- *Do something generous for someone else (send a thank you note, etc.)*

After you've practiced a new coping skill, check-in with yourself: how was your experience of trying a new coping skill? What was easier/harder than expected? Any surprises?

Links in a Chain is exercise that allows you to go back and review how you arrived at a certain outcome. For the purposes of Feast, often the behavior you'll be back tracking from is some form of disconnected eating but this process can be used for any undesirable behavior or consequence.

On the next page you'll see three graphics. The first is an explanation of what types of things go into each circle (or step). The second one is a sample Links in a Chain to show you how one might fill it out. The third graphic is blank for you to use.

THE **FIRST** CIRCLE IS WHERE YOU TAKE NOTE OF FACTORS THAT MIGHT HAVE MADE YOU MORE VULNERABLE TO SEQUENCE OF AND EVENTUAL OUTCOME OF EVENTS.

THE **SECOND** CIRCLE IS WHERE YOU'LL RECORD WHAT EVENT SET YOU OFF OR PROMPTED YOU TO TOWARD THE BEHAVIOR.

THE **THIRD** CIRCLE IS WHERE YOU'LL FLESH OUT THE CONNECTION BETWEEN THE TRIGGERING EVENT AND ACTION YOU TOOK. ITEMS IN THIS CIRCLE MIGHT BE CONSIDERED "OTHER CAUSAL FACTORS".

THE **FOURTH** CIRCLE IS THE UNDESIRABLE BEHAVIOR THAT YOU'RE WANTING TO EXPLORE.

THE **FIFTH** CIRCLE IS WHERE YOU NOTE ANY ALL OUTCOMES THAT RESULTED FROM YOUR BEHAVIOR.

Once you've completed a Chain you'll want to reflect on what you might do differently the next time and where in the chain there was a missed opportunity for self-care, deeper listening, reaching out for support, or other acts that might have better met your needs and resulted in fewer unwanted consequences.

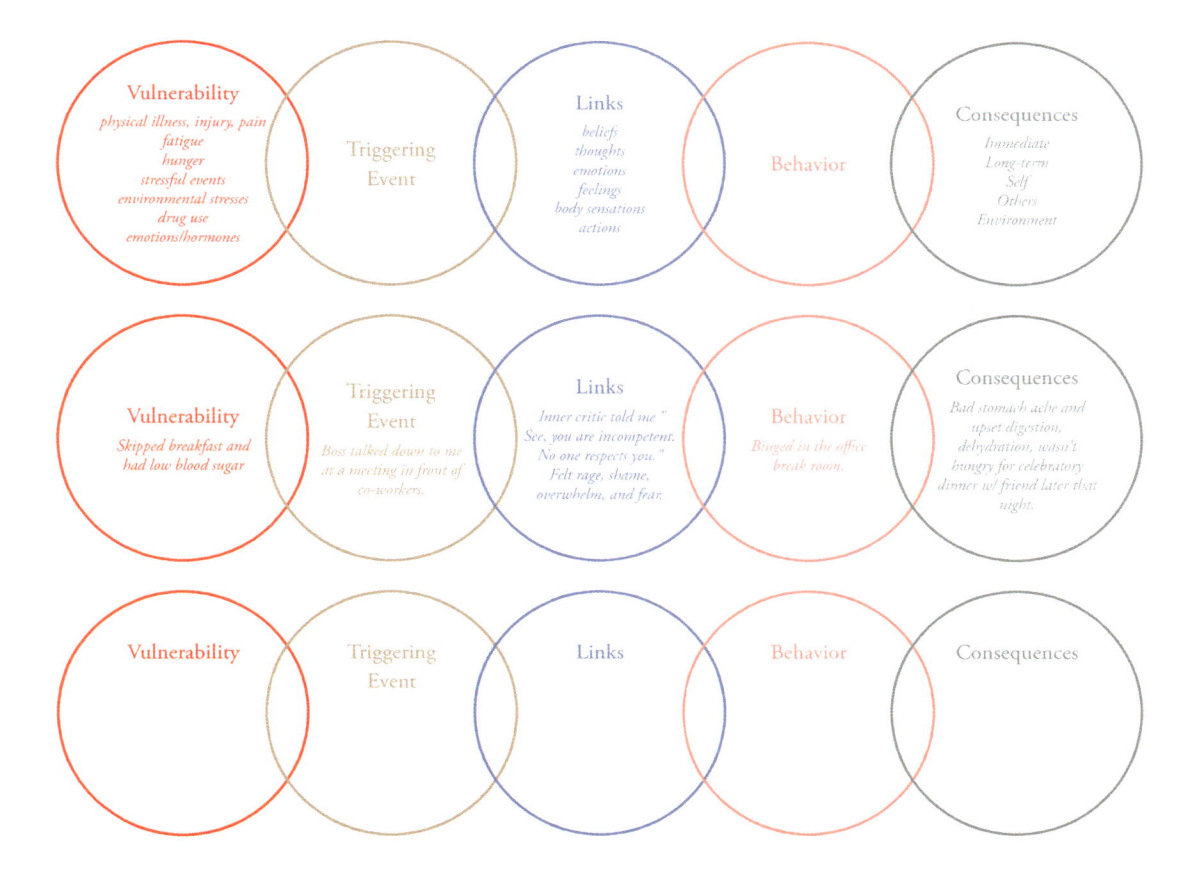

Vulnerability
physical illness, injury, pain
fatigue
hunger
stressful events
environmental stresses
drug use
emotions/hormones

Triggering Event

Links
beliefs
thoughts
emotions
feelings
body sensations
actions

Behavior

Consequences
Immediate
Long-term
Self
Others
Environment

Vulnerability
Skipped breakfast and had low blood sugar

Triggering Event
Boss talked down to me at a meeting in front of co-workers.

Links
Inner critic told me " See, you are incompetent. No one respects you." Felt rage, shame, overwhelm, and fear.

Behavior
Binged in the office break room.

Consequences
Bad stomach ache and upset digestion, dehydration, wasn't hungry for celebratory dinner w/ friend later that night.

Vulnerability

Triggering Event

Links

Behavior

Consequences

WEEK THREE

EXPERT INTERVIEWEE

Signe Darpinian

Signe Darpinian is a seasoned Licensed Marriage & Family Therapist with a Certificate in Eating Disorders and author of book *Knock Out Dieting: Create Peace Between You, Your Body, and Your Food* – a modern guide ideal for savvy women of all ages who are interested in the path to eating consciously, living presently, and eliminating dieting forever. She is the Founder and Executive Director of My Weigh, a Bay Area mindful and intuitive eating practice that provides a sanctuary from our culture's misguided messages around food and body image. In 2004, Signe also co-created Meghan's Place, a center for the treatment of clinical eating disorders and the only one of its kind in California's Central Valley.

Signe holds an M.A. in Counseling Psychology from San Francisco's John F. Kennedy University and a B.A. in Psychology from University of the Pacific. She is also the education chair for the Bay Area Chapter of the International Association of Eating Disorder Professionals (IAEDP). Over the past several years, she's been recognized by various organizations for her accomplishments in women's health and business while also continually requested for speaking engagements at renowned institutions like top-rated Rancho La Puerta Spa in Mexico.

Her insightful body of work has been featured in various newspapers, magazine and online sites. She's made several appearances on radio and television in northern California, including ABC7's talk show "The View from the Bay," the CBS-affiliate talk show "Bay Area Focus" with Emmy winner Susan Sikora, as well as The Lady Brain Show with Steph and Lauren.

With a deep dedication to continually developing breakthroughs in her field, Signe regularly participates in both national and global symposiums with the world's leading experts. Her greatest joy as a therapist is witnessing the natural unfolding process that clients experience as they disintegrate their judgemental stance around food symptoms and uncover deeper, actionable insights behind it all. Learn more about Signe and her work at *myweighfamilytherapy.com*.

NOTES

Want more?

Then check out these related posts that Rachel has written.

PAUSING FOR PEACE
goo.gl/W5XQyb

5 TRICKS FOR HEALING FROM EMOTIONAL AUTOIMMUNE DISORDERS
goo.gl/59u5wo

IN PRAISE OF ZOLOFT
goo.gl/ki9fIF

VANITY'S OTHER NAME
goo.gl/g0HzTF

WEEK THREE

NOTES

DAILY PRACTICE CHECKLIST

GENERAL *FEAST* SKILLS	S 8/14	M 8/15	T 8/16	W 8/17	Th 8/18	F 8/19	Sa 8/20
Meditated (on own or with recording)							
Read Feast Material							
Wrote responses to reflection questions							
Listened to expert interview/live call							
Reached out to the group for support							
Meditated (on own or with recording)							
Meditated (on own or with recording)							

SELF-COMPASSION SKILLS	S 8/14	M 8/15	T 8/16	W 8/17	Th 8/18	F 8/19	Sa 8/20
Spoke kindly to myself							
Acted self-compassionately toward myself							

WEEK THREE

CARE FOR SENSITIVE SOUL SKILLS	S 8/14	M 8/15	T 8/16	W 8/17	Th 8/18	F 8/19	Sa 8/20
Attempted to mangage my sensory input							
Advocated for my HSP needs							
Celebrated/observed my HSP strengths							

EFFECTIVE EMOTIONAL COPING SKILLS	S 8/14	M 8/15	T 8/16	W 8/17	Th 8/18	F 8/19	Sa 8/20
Paused!							
RAIN (recognize, allow, investigate, natural awareness)							
Made a concious choice to distract							
Urge surfed							
Reached out to the group for support							
Did cost/benefit analysis							
Went in slo-mo							

WEEK FOUR

Integration Week

———

THE FOUNDATION

WEEK FOUR

> ## Reminder!
>
> This week please read Forward – Chapter 5 and Chapter 7 in *Intuitive Eating*.

The integration weeks can be just as powerful as our more active weeks if you take advantage of the time. Here are a few tips:

1. Schedule time to review the material. Make a few dates with yourself. Go to your favorite cafe. Put on bright lipstick. Review. Reflect. Journal. Discuss with your buddy. Let it all sink in even deeper.

2. PRACTICE. PRACTICE. PRACTICE. Use your new skills. Be awkward at them. Practice anyway. Practice at work. Practice with your friends and families. Practice.

3. Get some fresh air and time in nature. Nothing feeds the soul and brings us back to ourselves and out of our heads like a good walk through the woods or stroll along the beach. Get yourself to the nearest tree and marvel at how much it trusts itself.

4. Trust the process. It's easy when we're in an integration week to hear your inner critic and fear voices get louder. You're in a new land and you don't have a complete map. Trust that Feast and Rachel are holding you. Trust that you are right where you need to be.

Back next week!

INTUITIVE EATING QUESTIONS / FORWARD THROUGH CHAPTER FIVE AND SEVEN

On page 2 and 3 the authors outline the symptoms of "Dieting Backlash", do you see yourself as having any of these symptoms. If so, which ones and how do they show up in your life?

In Chapters One and Two the following words and phrases appear when discussing dieting: trap, set up to fail, weary, futile, war, obsessed, sinful, battle cry, punishable, paroled, life sentence, police, mafia, desperate, interrogate, anguish, vigilant, chastising, shackles, and prison. Reflect on what this collection of words stirs in you.

In Chapter Two the authors define several 'personality types' of eaters. What type are you? Are you a hybrid of several types?

At the bottom of page 19 begins a quiz to help you determine if you're an Intuitive Eater. Take the quiz and reflect on your answers.

WEEK FOUR

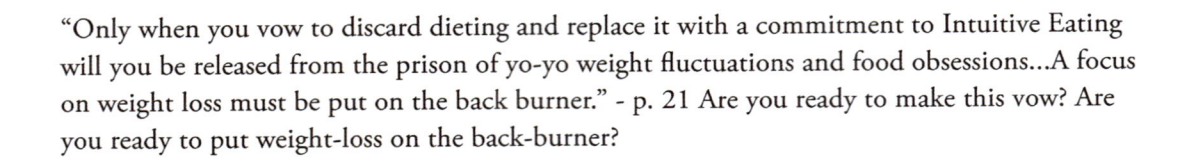

"Only when you vow to discard dieting and replace it with a commitment to Intuitive Eating will you be released from the prison of yo-yo weight fluctuations and food obsessions...A focus on weight loss must be put on the back burner." - p. 21 Are you ready to make this vow? Are you ready to put weight-loss on the back-burner?

Starting on page 48, the physical, emotional, and psychological damage of dieting is outlined. Have you experienced any of these consequences? If so, which ones?

Starting on page 51, in the "Forget Being Obedient" section, the authors illuminate how diets violate our boundaries and thus inspire rebellion. Can you relate to this? If so, explain:

I find it helpful to transcribe passages that resonate. It somehow helps them 'stick' better and allows me to go back and find them. Use this space to capture your favorite lines or passages from this week's readings:

FORWARD:

CHAPTER ONE:

CHAPTER TWO:

CHAPTER THREE

WEEK FOUR

CHAPTER FOUR:

CHAPTER FIVE:

CHAPTER SEVEN:

Did this week's reading assignment leave you with any questions?

THE HAES MANIFESTO

Written by Dr. Linda Bacon

HEALTH AT EVERY SIZE: THE NEW PEACE MOVEMENT

We're losing the war on obesity. Fighting fat has not made the fat go away. However, extensive "collateral damage" has resulted: Food and body preoccupation, self-hatred, eating disorders, weight cycling, weight discrimination, poor health. . . . Few of us are at peace with our bodies, whether because we're fat or because we fear becoming fat. It's time to withdraw the troops. There is a compassionate alternative to the war—Health at Every Size—which has proven to be much more successful at health improvement—and without the unwanted side effects.[1, 2] The scientific research consistently shows that common assumptions underlying the war on obesity just don't stand up to the evidence.

ASSUMPTION: "OVERWEIGHT" AND "OBESE" PEOPLE DIE SOONER THAN LEANER PEOPLE.

False! Almost all epidemiologic studies indicate people in the overweight or moderately obese categories live at least as long— or longer—than people in the normal weight category. The most comprehensive review of the research pooled data from 26 studies and found overweight to be associated with greater longevity than normal weight.[3] Analysis of the National Health and Nutrition Examination Surveys I, II, and III, which followed the largest nationally representative cohort of U.S. adults, also determined that the "ideal" weight for longevity was in the "overweight" category.[4]

ASSUMPTION: BEING "OVERWEIGHT" OR "OBESE" PUTS PEOPLE AT SIGNIFICANT HEALTH RISK.

False! Epidemiological studies rarely acknowledge factors like fitness, activity, nutrient intake, weight cycling, or socioeconomic status when considering connections between weight and disease. Yet all play a role. When studies do control for these factors, increased risk of disease disappears or is significantly reduced.[5] What's likely going on here is that these other factors increase disease risk at the same time they increase the risk of weight gain.

ASSUMPTION: ANYONE WHO IS DETERMINED CAN LOSE WEIGHT AND KEEP IT OFF.

False! The vast majority of people who try to lose weight regain it, regardless of whether they maintain their diet or exercise program.[6,7]

This occurs in all studies, no matter how many calories or what proportions of fat, protein or carbohydrates are used in the diet, or what types of exercise programs are pursued. Many studies also show that dieting is a strong predictor of future weight gain.[8-14]

ASSUMPTION: WEIGHT LOSS WILL PROLONG LIFE.

False! No one has ever shown that losing weight prolongs life. Some studies actually indicate that intentional weight loss increases the risk of dying early from certain diseases.[15-20]

ASSUMPTION: THE ONLY WAY FOR "OVERWEIGHT" PEOPLE TO IMPROVE HEALTH IS TO LOSE WEIGHT.

False! Most health indicators can be improved through changing health behaviors, regardless of whether weight is lost.[5] For example, lifestyle changes can reduce blood pressure, largely or completely independent of changes in body weight.[1, 21, 22] The same can be said for blood lipids.[1, 23, 24] Improvements in insulin sensitivity and blood lipids as a result of aerobic exercise training have been documented even in persons who actually gained body fat while participating in the intervention.[24, 25]

ASSUMPTION: HEALTH IS DECLINING AS A RESULT OF AN "OBESITY EPIDEMIC."

False! While it's true that we're moderately fatter than we used to be, life expectancy has increased dramatically during the same time period in which our weight rose (from 70.8 years in 1970 to 77.8 years in 2005).[26] That's right, government statistics predict that the average kid can now expect to live almost eight years longer than his or her parents! Not only are we living longer than ever before, but we're healthier than ever and chronic disease is appearing much later in life.[26] Death rates attributed to heart disease have steadily declined throughout the entire spike in obesity.[27] Both the World Health Organization and the Social Security Administration project life expectancy to continue to rise in coming decades.[28, 29] We are simply not seeing the catastrophic consequences predicted to result from the "obesity epidemic."

BLAME ECONOMICS

Why do these faulty assumptions continue to proliferate and why isn't the reality more widely known? There can only be one explanation when science so blatantly contradicts popular thought: economics.

There is a huge industry that benefits from widening the boundaries of what is considered a problematic weight, including weight loss centers, supplement makers, drug companies, physicians, and purveyors of diet books, foods and programs. Even scientists benefit by getting research grants and serving as consultants, or by running weight loss centers at universities. Convincing us of a crisis can also aid government agencies in obtaining congressional funding. And expert panels that create public policy and determine research funding are populated by individuals with financial conflicts of interests.

That said, I do not believe that those engaging in this damaging paradigm are part of a widespread conspiracy. We are all raised with the assumption that fat is bad and permanent weight loss can be achieved through dietary change and exercise. These assumptions are so strongly a part of our cultural landscape that they are regarded as self-evident, and few even consider questioning them. As a result, many well-intentioned, caring people unknowingly collude and transmit this cultural bias. Also, there is little reward for questioning these assumptions, other than peace of mind. Indeed, for a professional to challenge these ideas is tantamount to career suicide; this is in stark contrast to the large financial/status incentive for supporting the old paradigm.

WHAT CAN YOU DO?

Refuse to fight in an unjust war. Join the new peace movement: "Health at Every Size" (HAES). HAES acknowledges that well-being and healthy habits are more important than any number on the scale. Participating is simple:

> 1. **ACCEPT YOUR SIZE.** Love and appreciate the body you have. Self-acceptance empowers you to move on and make positive changes.

2. TRUST YOURSELF. We all have internal systems designed to keep us healthy—and at a healthy weight. Support your body in naturally finding its appropriate weight by honoring its signals of hunger, fullness, and appetite.

3. ADOPT HEALTHY LIFESTYLE HABITS. Develop and nurture connections with others and look for purpose and meaning in your life. Fulfilling your social, emotional, and spiritual needs restores food to its rightful place as a source of nourishment and pleasure.

- Find the joy in moving your body and becoming more physically vital in your everyday life.
- Eat when you're hungry, stop when you're full, and seek out pleasurable and satisfying foods.
- Tailor your tastes so that you enjoy more nutritious foods, staying mindful that there is plenty of room for less nutritious choices in the context of an overall healthy diet and lifestyle.

4. EMBRACE SIZE DIVERSITY. Humans come in a variety of sizes and shapes. Open to the beauty found across the spectrum and support others in recognizing their unique attractiveness.

REFERENCES

1. Bacon, L., et al., Size acceptance and intuitive eating improve health for obese, female chronic dieters. Journal of the American Dietetic Association, 2005. 105: p. 929-36.
2. Provencher, V., et al., Health-at-every-size and eating behaviors: 1-year follow-up results of a size acceptance intervention. J Am Diet Assoc, 2009. 109(11): p. 1854-61.
3. McGee, D.L., Body mass index and mortality: a meta-analysis based on person-level data from twenty-six observational studies. Annals of Epidemiology, 2005. 15(2): p. 87-97.
4. Flegal, K.M., et al., Excess deaths associated with underweight, overweight, and obesity. Journal of the American Medical Association, 2005. 293(15): p. 1861-7.
5. Campos, P., et al., The epidemiology of overweight and obesity:

public health crisis or moral panic? International Journal of Epidemiology, 2005.

6. Miller, W.C., How effective are traditional dietary and exercise interventions for weight loss? Medicine and Science in Sports and Exercise, 1999. 31(8): p. 1129-1134.

7. Mann, T., et al., Medicare's Search for Effective Obesity Treatments: Diets Are Not the Answer. American Psychologist, 2007. 62(3): p. 220-33.

8. Stice, E., et al., Naturalistic weight-reduction efforts prospectively predict growth in relative weight and onset of obesity among female adolescents. Journal of Consulting and Clinical Psychology, 1999. 67: p. 967-974.

9. Stice, E., K. Presnell, and H. Shaw, Psychological and Behavioral-Risk Factors for Obesity Onset in Adolescent Girls: A Prospective-Study. Journal of Consulting and Clinical Psychology, 2005. 73(2): p. 195-202.

10. Coakley, E.H., et al., Predictors of weight change in men: Results from the Health Professionals Follow-Up Study. International Journal of Obesity and Related Metabolic Disorders, 1998. 22: p. 89-96.

11. Bild, D.E., et al., Correlates and predictors of weight loss in young adults: The CARDIA study. International Journal of Obesity and Related Metabolic Disorders, 1996. 20(1): p. 47-55.

12. French, S.A., et al., Predictors of weight change over two years among a population of working adults: The Healthy Worker Project. International Journal of Obesity, 1994. 18: p. 145-154.

13. Korkeila, M., et al., Weight-loss attempts and risk of major weight gain. American Journal of Clinical Nutrition, 1999. 70: p. 965-973.

14. Shunk, J.A. and L.L. Birch, Girls at risk for overweight at age 5 are at risk for dietary restraint, disinhibited overeating, weight concerns, and greater weight gain from 5 to 9 years. Journal of the American Dietetic Association, 2004. 104(7): p. 1120-6.

15. Williamson, D.F., et al., Prospective study of intentional weight loss and mortality in never-smoking overweight U.S. white women aged 40-64 years. American Journal of Epidemiology, 1995. 141: p. 1128-1141.

16. Williamson, D.F., et al., Prospective study of intentional weight loss and mortality in overweight white men aged 40-64 years. American Journal of Epidemiology, 1999. 149(6): p. 491-503.

17. Andres, R., D.C. Muller, and J.D. Sorkin, Long-term effects of change in body weight on all-cause mortality. A review. Annals of

Internal Medicine, 1993. 119: p. 737-743.
18. Yaari, S. and U. Goldbourt, Voluntary and involuntary weight loss: associations with long term mortality in 9,228 middle-aged and elderly men. American Journal of Epidemiology, 1998. 148: p. 546-55.
19. Gaesser, G., Thinness and weight loss: Beneficial or detrimental to longevity. Medicine and Science in Sports and Exercise, 1999. 31(8): p. 1118-1128.
20. Sørensen, T., et al., Intention to lose weight, weight changes, and 18-y mortality in overweight individuals without co-morbidities. PLoS Med, 2005. 2: p. E171.
21. Fagard, R.H., Physical activity in the prevention and treatment of hypertension in the obese. Med Sci Sports Exerc, 1999. 31(11 Suppl): p. S624-30.
22. Appel, L.J., et al., A clinical trial of the effects of dietary patterns on blood pressure. New England Journal of Medicine, 1997. 33: p. 1117-1124.
23. Kraus, W.E., et al., Effects of the amount and intensity of exercise on plasma lipoproteins. N Engl J Med, 2002. 347(19): p. 1483-92.
24. Lamarche, B., et al., Is body fat loss a determinant factor in the improvement of carbohydrate and lipid metabolism following aerobic exercise training in obese women? Metabolism, 1992. 41: p. 1249-1256.
25. Bjorntorp, P., et al., The effect of physical training on insulin production in obesity. Metabolism, 1970. 19: p. 631-638.
26. National Center for Health Statistics, Health, United States, 2007. With Chartbook on Trends in the Health of Americans. 2007, Hyattsville, MD.
27. Rosamond, W., et al., Heart Disease and Stroke Statistics 2008 Update. A Report From the American Heart Association Statistics Committee and Stroke Statistics Subcommittee. Circulation, 2007.
28. Mathers, C. and D. Loncar, Projections of Global Mortality and Burden of Disease from 2002 to 2030. PLoS Med, 2006. 3(11): p. 2011-2029.
29. Social Security Administration, *Periodic Life Table*. 2007 (updated 7/9/07).

Excerpt from *Health at Every Size: The Surprising Truth About Your Weight*
© 2010 by Linda Bacon. More info at www.HAESbook.com.

WEEK FOUR

NOTES

NOTES

WEEK FOUR

NOTES

SETTING THE TABLE

Often when we leave behind the false comfort and safety of diets it can feel like the ground has dropped out beneath us. Without the strict rules and clear line of good and bad or right and wrong, what's a woman to do/eat/wear/think/feel?

Chapter 4 in *Intuitive Eating* is an essential foundation for the road ahead because it gives you some lay of the land. Please review this chapter to get a sense of the stages of this journey.

As many of you know by now, my own journey to becoming an intuitive eater—wherein it feels natural and I rarely think about it—took years. At least two years to feel solid and more than that to feel integrated. So the three months of *Feast* and the two months ahead of us are just the beginning (or a continuation if you've been traveling for a while). This isn't a bad thing and certainly not a reason to fret, it's simply important to know that you may be early on this journey.

"...your journey back to Intuitive Eating depends on how long you've been dieting, how strongly entrenched your diet thinking is, how long you've been using food to cope with life, how willing you are to trust yourself, and how willing you are to put weight on the back burner and learning to become an Intuitive Eater the primary goal."

INTUITIVE EATING, PAGE 31

It's also important to know that the journey that lies ahead of us is not linear. You will not spend the next seven weeks with things getting progressively easier. Sorry. We're entering into a period of practice and when we practice new things, we never master them right out of the gate.

My hope is that you won't fear falling down. That you won't give up if you're going all happily and then suddenly find yourself back at the starting line. THIS IS NORMAL.

I also expect that you may feel overwhelmed a few times in the weeks ahead. Not by the material but just by being a beginner and by being more engaged in aspects of your life than in the past. Again, THIS IS NORMAL. If you find yourself overwhelmed, greet it as a friend you expected to see. "Hello, overwhelm. Rachel said you'd be stopping by…"

Remember, I've been where you are. I'm holding this space for you to try new things, be awkward, get lost, and always always begin again.

Rachel

WEEK FIVE

Honoring Hunger & Fullness

AT THE TABLE

THE WAITING GAME

When I began my recovery from anorexia 13 years ago, I knew I had a long road ahead. I lacked the most basic of skills: how to tell when I was hungry, and when I was full.

I grew up with a dad who practiced, "If it tastes good, eat more," spent my free time dabbling in diets, and eventually developed a full-blown eating disorder. I had no clue what hunger or fullness felt like. No clue.

I did know that I could relearn what it felt like to be hungry and full, or at least I had faith that I could. I knew others had relearned after years of disconnection. Why couldn't I?

I knew that if I paid attention long enough, and didn't derail myself by judging myself, I could relearn how to hear my body's hunger and fullness cues again.

I was in college at the time, and had a few particularly supportive friends. One day, while eating lunch in the dining hall with my friend Erin, she finished eating and I realized I didn't know if I was done. I honestly didn't know if I was full, or if I wanted to eat more.

I said, "Would you wait with me? I just need to sit here a bit longer until I can tell if I'm full, or still hungry." That's the thing about relearning; it requires that we slow down. I know that it's not always possible in our day-to-day lives to spend tons of extra time at meals, but over the next few months I hope you'll grant yourself a free pass to take the time you need to listen inward while you're eating. You are in a special, intensive healing phase, and it's OK, necessary even, to prioritize yourself more than ever.

Erin did sit with me. We sat there long after the lunch crowd had cleared out. We sat while the cleaning crew came in and the kitchen staff got to work on dinner. We sat waiting for me to get more information from my body. We sat until I was ready to either eat more, or leave. That moment in the dining hall is what it took for me to begin hearing my hunger and fullness cues again.

In the beginning, I wasn't always patient, and I didn't hit the mark most of the time. That first year of recovery was filled with a lot of belly aches (when I missed a cue that I was full) and second dinners (when I missed a cue that I was hungry), but I just kept paying attention and recalibrating as best I could. Slowly, slowly, slowly, it became easier to know when I was hungry, and when I was full.

This isn't like riding a bike where you might ride down the street with ease on your first try; this is a two steps forward, one step back process. Every time we hear a hunger cue, or a fullness cue and we honor it, we celebrate. Every time we miss a cue, we meet ourselves with compassion and reflect on what happened so that it can help us the next time. This is the practice.

It won't be smooth sailing at the start, so please, be gentle with yourself.

"BUT, BUT, BUT . . ."

But I don't have any idea when I'm hungry.

Of course not! You've spent many years overriding, ignoring, and judging the call for food. The good news is that it's never, ever too late to reestablish this connection with yourself, relearn the physical sensations, and rebuild trust. You're primed to practice right where you are.

But I'm always hungry.

Unless you have a very, very rare medical condition, I have to disagree, but I might be able to help you understand what's going on:

- If you've been restricting, are medically underweight, or are below your SET POINT WEIGHT ↘, you might be underfed, and have some "hunger debt." This is easily resolved with a consistent, sufficient intake of food. If you want a referral to an Intuitive Eating nutritionist to help with this, I have many.

- If you're not enjoying what you're eating, not eating what you really want, or not eating what you enjoy, you won't find satiety easily. Eating what we want and what tastes good leads to our body's feeling full. Ask yourself as you're eating, "Am I eating what I want and what I really enjoy? Am I paying attention while I eat so that I can receive enjoyment?"

- If you're using food to cope with a persistently stressful situation, or starvation in another area of your life (e.g. career, relationship), you may find yourself constantly craving the numbing. This is a good opportunity to use the skills from week three (Effective Emotional Coping) and begin to differentiate between true hunger and "coping'" hunger.

> **SET POINT WEIGHT**
> *is the narrow weight range at which an individual's internal "weight thermostat" is set. It is determined by a confluence of factors including genetics, age, and past dieting activity. When the body falls below the set point weight, the body seeks to restore the weight though increased hunger and decreased metabolism. Chronic yo-yo dieting can drive up a person's set point weight.*

But I don't want to stop when I'm full, that feels like a diet. I don't want to stop eating.

When you are on a diet, the expert lives outside of you, and tells you when and what to eat. On the well-fed woman's path, you are the expert. No one will tell you to start or stop eating. You can eat till the cows come home. Our body is designed to tell us when it has had enough, and when it needs more.

You never have to stop eating, but we want you to have a choice. We want you to feel like you could stop eating because you know you can eat again, anytime. The more you honor these signals, both hunger and fullness, the sooner you'll find yourself free from food obsession. Trust me.

The bottom line is that there is nothing for you to rebel against. You do not have to do anything. You get to give yourself the experience of listening to your body because it's ultimately what feels good, and what enables you to enjoy the most out of life, including food.

But if let myself eat when I'm hungry I'll never stop eating.

> **Reminder!**
>
> This week please read Chapters Six and Nine in *Intuitive Eating*.

This is a common belief, but also is not true. As soon as you recondition your brain to know that there will always be enough (and this takes time), you will find that you don't have any desire to eat more than is comfortable, and your fullness will arrive on schedule. It is the mental state of impending restriction that drives overconsumption, not you, not some lack of willpower, not some bag of chips.

If this "but" resonates for you, you can read more about it in my blog post, *"The Illusion of the Bottomless Pit"* found here: *rachelwcole.com/2014/05/24/the-illusion-of-the-bottomless-pit*.

But if I let myself eat when I'm hungry, I'll eat at random times (lunch at 9 AM, dinner at 4 PM). I'll be way off schedule.

When you start to listen to your body, and let it eat what it wants, your eating habits may change, and that's OK. You may find that you eat more or less frequently, larger or smaller quantities, and new or the same food. To the extent that your life permits, let yourself eat when you're hungry and stop when you're full, even if that means eating at different times, in different quantities, or different foods. You aren't locked into 8 AM breakfast, 1 PM lunch, and 6 PM dinner unless that's what your body wants. Remember, there are no rules!

If you live with a significant other, or family members who you typically share meals with, give yourself permission to eat separately from them. You need the space and freedom to be able to eat before they eat dinner if you're hungry, or after they eat dinner if you're full. You can still join them at the table and engage in conversation. Explain that you're practicing eating when you're hungry and stopping when you're full. We can discuss this more on Thursday's call.

THE PRACTICE

This week is a little different because I'm giving you a bit of your Wednesday challenge early. I'm doing this because you're ready to start practicing. You can start right now. Your tool is this Hunger-Fullness Scale (I like this one better than the one in the book, but either works).

I want you to approach this with a lot of curiosity. Simply notice for a few days, without putting too much pressure on yourself, are you eating when you're hungry? Are you stopping when you're full? Do you let yourself get too hungry, or too full? Your task is to notice the ebb and flow with the intention, when you're aware of it, to eat more often when you're hungry, and stop more often when you've had enough.

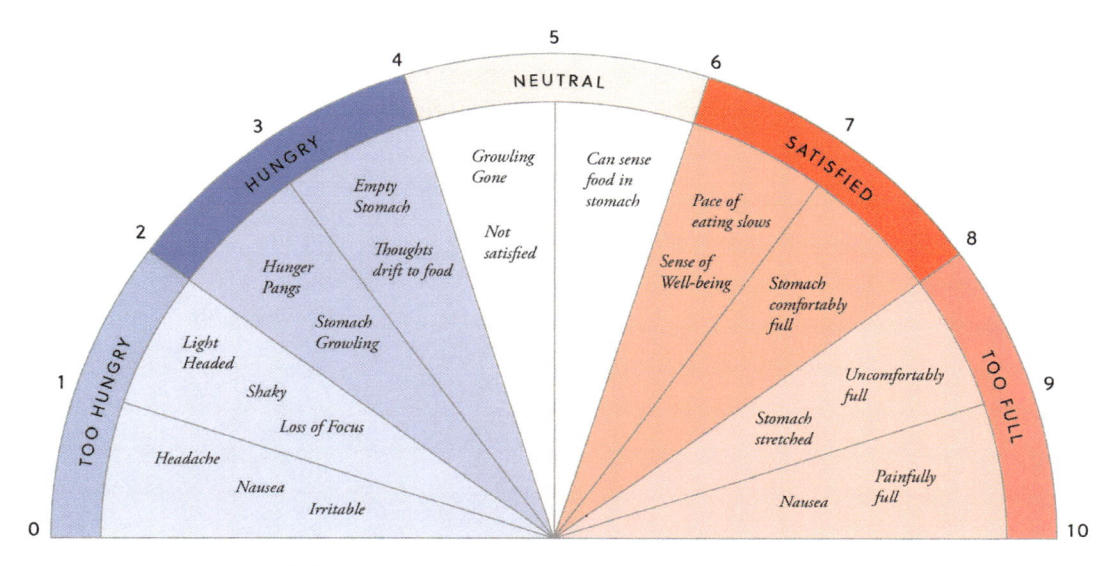

(Source: Green Mountain at Fox Run)

A FEW HELPFUL TIDBITS & REMINDERS

IT'S NOT JUST WHEN YOU EAT; IT'S ALSO WHAT YOU EAT.
The more you let yourself eat what you want, the easier it will be to find freedom and ease with food, and experience awareness of your body's cues.

PAY ATTENTION.
You can call it "mindful eating" if you want, but that sounds too serious to me and like no fun at all! I prefer to call it "paying attention." When you pay attention, you get to actually experience the joy of eating. Food is delicious, especially when it's what we want and we are hungry, so why not show up fully for it? In order to hear your hunger and fullness cues, pay as much attention as you can to what your body is saying.

SLOW DOWN.
The slower you go, the more opportunities you'll have to catch your hunger and fullness cues before you speed past them. Sometimes the difference between hungry and starving is twenty minutes. Sometimes the difference between full and too full is three bites. Going slowly really helps. It allows you to really taste and enjoy your food. You deserve this most basic right: to enjoy your food.

REMEMBER THAT NORMAL EATING IS IMPERFECT EATING.

Learning to honor our hunger and fullness cues is not about becoming a robot. Normal eaters overeat and undereat at times, but for the most part, they don't judge themselves. As family therapist, and feeding and eating specialist, Ellyn Satter, (*ellynsatterinstitute.org/hte/whatisnormaleating.php*) reminds us:

Normal eating is going to the table hungry and eating until you are satisfied. It is being able to choose food you like and eat it and truly get enough of it, not just stop eating because you think you should. Normal eating is being able to give some thought to your food selection so you get nutritious food, but not being so wary and restrictive that you miss out on enjoyable food. Normal eating is giving yourself permission to eat sometimes because you are happy, sad or bored, or just because it feels good. Normal eating is mostly three meals a day, or four or five, or it can be choosing to munch along the way. It is leaving some cookies on the plate because you know you can have some again tomorrow, or it is eating more now because they taste so wonderful. Normal eating is overeating at times, feeling stuffed and uncomfortable. And it can be undereating at times and wishing you had more. Normal eating is trusting your body to make up for your mistakes in eating. Normal eating takes up some of your time and attention, but keeps its place as only one important area of your life.

In short, normal eating is flexible. It varies in response to your hunger, your schedule, your proximity to food and your feelings.

A final note on this week's topic:

More than anything, honoring our hunger and fullness cues is an act of respect and tenderness. It is not a violent act, like dieting. You are not the enemy. Your body is not the enemy. Your appetite is not the enemy. Food is not the enemy.

Honoring our body's wishes is one of the key steps toward establishing lasting internal peace. It is an acknowledgement that, "Yes, body, we're on the same team and I trust you."

WEEK FIVE

REFLECTIONS ON HONORING HUNGER & FULLNESS

What does your body feel like when it's starving? What physical symptoms tell you it's past time to eat?

What does your body feel like when it's hungry? What physical symptoms tell you it's time to eat?

What does your body feel like when it's satisfied or full? What physical symptoms tell you you've had enough food?

What does your body feel like when it's overstuffed? What physical symptoms tell you you've eaten more food than is comfortable?

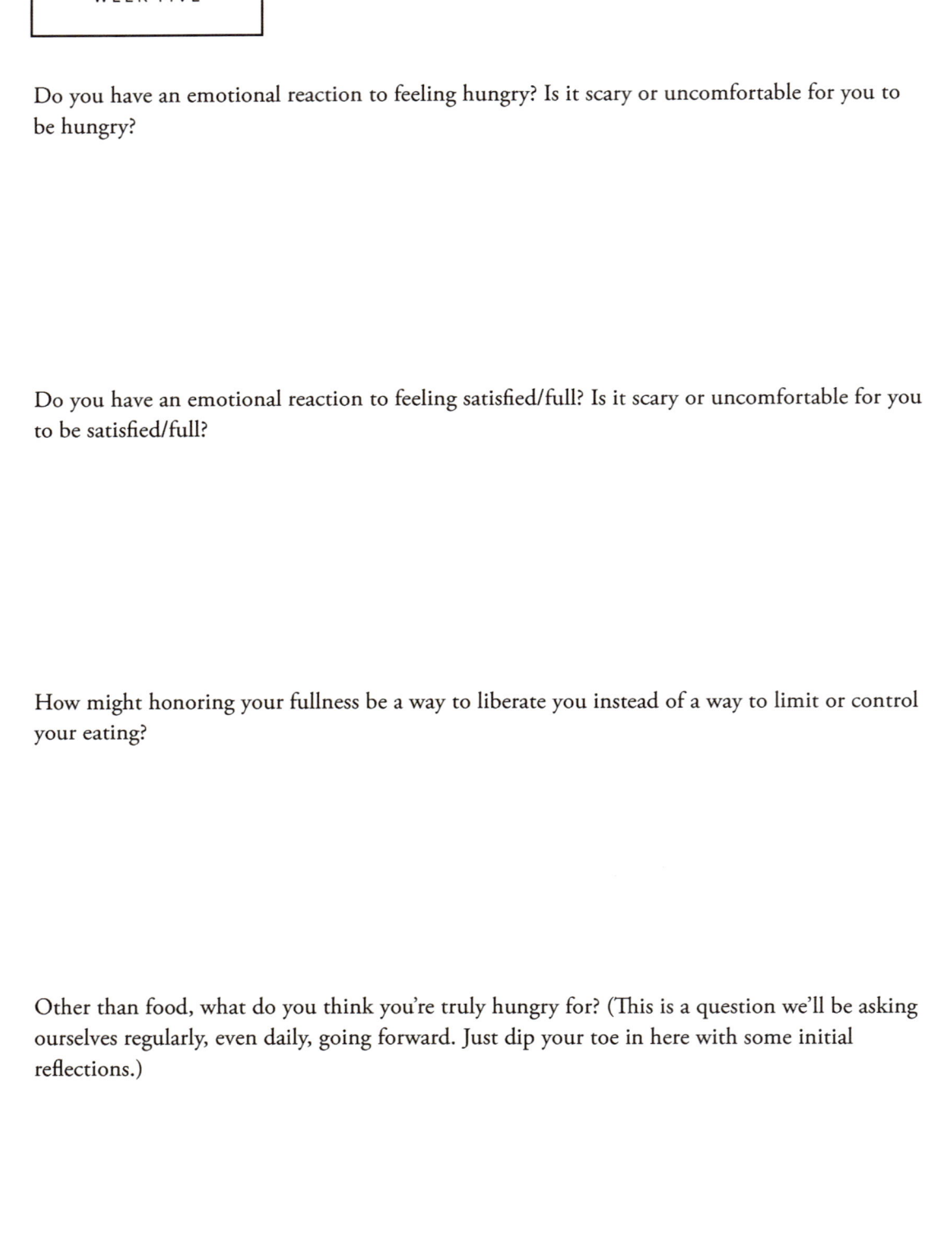

WEEK FIVE

Do you have an emotional reaction to feeling hungry? Is it scary or uncomfortable for you to be hungry?

Do you have an emotional reaction to feeling satisfied/full? Is it scary or uncomfortable for you to be satisfied/full?

How might honoring your fullness be a way to liberate you instead of a way to limit or control your eating?

Other than food, what do you think you're truly hungry for? (This is a question we'll be asking ourselves regularly, even daily, going forward. Just dip your toe in here with some initial reflections.)

INTUITIVE EATING QUESTIONS / CHAPTER SIX AND NINE

In Chapter Six, which line or passage was the most powerful? Transcribe here:

In Chapter Nine, which line or passage was the most powerful? Transcribe here:

Did this week's reading assignment leave you with any questions?

WEEK FIVE

HONORING HUNGER & FULLNESS CHALLENGE

Practice using this Hunger-Fullness Scale each day this week and going forward for the duration of *Feast*. The goal is not to be perfect or to use this scale as a means for harshly judging yourself. All normal eaters eat past full or neglect to eat until they are ravenous sometimes. The goal for you is to use this tool to bring more awareness to your eating habits and to help you eat more often when you are hungry and to honor when you are full.

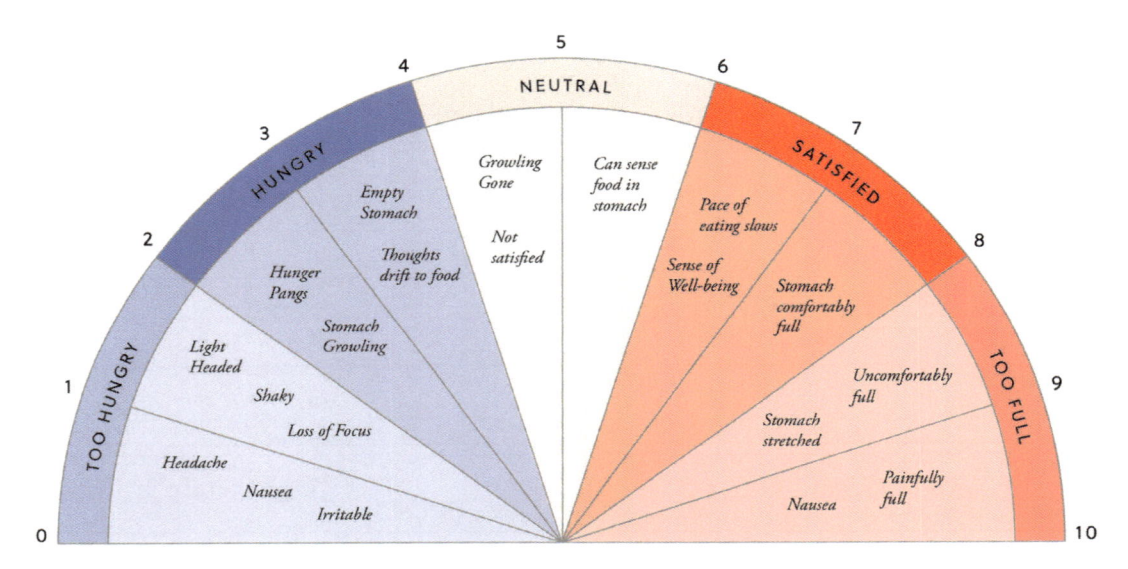

(Source: Green Mountain at Fox Run)

To start you want to be checking in with where you are on this scale regularly — every hour if possible. Consider setting alarms on your phone to remind you to pause and check in to see where you fall on the scale.

Use this space to reflect upon your experience with the Hunger-Fullness Scale. What do you notice? What patterns do you see? Any surprises?

WEEK FIVE

EXPERT INTERVIEWEE

Tracy Brown

Tracy Brown shares insight and expertise she has accumulated throughout her extensive career as a clinical care leader. For the past 9 years Tracy has devoted her life to helping individuals with eating disorders and diet-trauma to live happier, more embodied lives. An edge walker as a dietitian, incorporating body, mind and essence into her sessions, she delights in seeing her clients learn to be their own "nutrition experts" as they decode how what's going on on their plate is what is happening in their internal life and mirrored in the external. Tracy holds a Bachelors of Science in Dietetics and Nutrition from Southern Illinois University and completed a 2-year Eating Disorder Training Program with Karin Kratina, PhD, RD, LD/N.

NOTES

Want more?

Then check out these related posts that Rachel has written.

THE PENDULUM
goo.gl/eLGjCx

THE ILLUSION OF THE BOTTOMLESS PIT
goo.gl/XTrKbT

THE SPIRAL CLIMB
goo.gl/ESjgl5

DIETING IS A VIOLENT ACT
goo.gl/1RazpY

SOLA DOSIS FACIT VENENUM
goo.gl/pjOpaJ

DEFINING WHAT WORKS
goo.gl/35HTR3

TAKE BACK YOUR LIFE
goo.gl/nQjadX

A WORLD GONE MAD
goo.gl/tCMnoo

WEEK FIVE

NOTES

NOTES

WEEK FIVE

DAILY PRACTICE CHECKLIST

GENERAL *FEAST* SKILLS	S 8/28	M 8/29	T 8/30	W 8/31	Th 9/1	F 9/2	Sa 9/3
Meditated (on own or with recording)							
Read Feast Material							
Wrote responses to reflection questions							
Listened to expert interview/live call							
Reached out to the group for support							
Meditated (on own or with recording)							
Meditated (on own or with recording)							

SELF-COMPASSION SKILLS	S 8/28	M 8/29	T 8/30	W 8/31	Th 9/1	F 9/2	Sa 9/3
Spoke kindly to myself							
Acted self-compassionately toward myself							

CARE FOR SENSITIVE SOUL SKILLS	S 8/28	M 8/29	T 8/30	W 8/31	F 9/2	F 3/5	Sa 9/3
Attempted to mangage my sensory input							
Advocated for my HSP needs							
Celebrated/observed my HSP strengths							

EFFECTIVE EMOTIONAL COPING SKILLS	S 8/28	M 8/29	T 8/30	W 8/31	F 9/2	F 3/5	Sa 9/3
Paused!							
RAIN (recognize, allow, investigate, natural awareness)							
Made a concious choice to distract							
Urge surfed							
Reached out to the group for support							
Did cost/benefit analysis							
Went in slo-mo							

WEEK FIVE

HUNGER/FULLNESS SKILLS	S 8/28	M 8/29	T 8/30	W 8/31	Th 9/1	F 9/2	Sa 9/3
Recognized bodily cues re: hunger/fullness							
Honored bodily cues re: hunger/fullness							
Used the hunger-fullness scale							
Ate when I was hungry (before starving)							
Stopped when I was satisfied (before stuffed)							

WEEK SIX

Eating Freely

―――

AT THE TABLE

CHASING PURITY

When I moved to California to get an MA in Holistic Health Education, I had already been awakened to *Health at Every Size*, and broken free from the dieter's mindset, or so I thought.

My new California lifestyle turned out to be a fierce cocktail of food "shoulds"' and "shouldn'ts," none of which looked like the food rules I'd attempted to follow in the past. The result was that they easily snuck in under my radar. I combined the Bay Area's culture of, "Eat local!" "Eat organic!" "Eat what's in season!" with my graduate school's promotion of eating systems based on Chinese medicine, Ayurveda, and Weston A. Price.

None of the West Coast "natural food" culture registered to me as a diet at the time, and I paid the price. I spent many years struggling with orthorexia, even longer than I struggled with anorexia, and I didn't even know it, because I so strongly identified as "healed" when it came to my eating disorder.

> **Reminder!**
>
> This week please read Chapter Eight in *Intuitive Eating*.

During this time, food wasn't about pleasure, it wasn't even about my weight; it was about purity. Looking back now, I can see that how I ate had all the hallmarks of a diet:

- *Someone else was the expert (e.g. professors, farmers, authors, food scientists).*
- *There was "good" and "bad" food, and a "right" and "wrong" way to eat.*
- *My body's wishes were consistently being ignored and overridden.*
- *It made me less anxious to follow the various eating "rules."*

On my path to recovery from orthorexia, it would have been so easy to flip the switch on my puritanical ways and swing over to a world of eating "junk" food 24/7. I could have totally said, "Fuck it," but that wouldn't have set me free.

Freedom came from stepping into the autonomous role of expert and knowing that I am the one who knows best what's right for me. Freedom came from stepping into being someone who made choices rather than dogmatically followed the rules, or immaturely rebelled. Freedom came from eating in a way that brought me closer to myself, not farther away.

ME? KNOW BEST?

Three factors converge that make it incredibly hard to trust that we can be the experts on how to best feed ourselves.

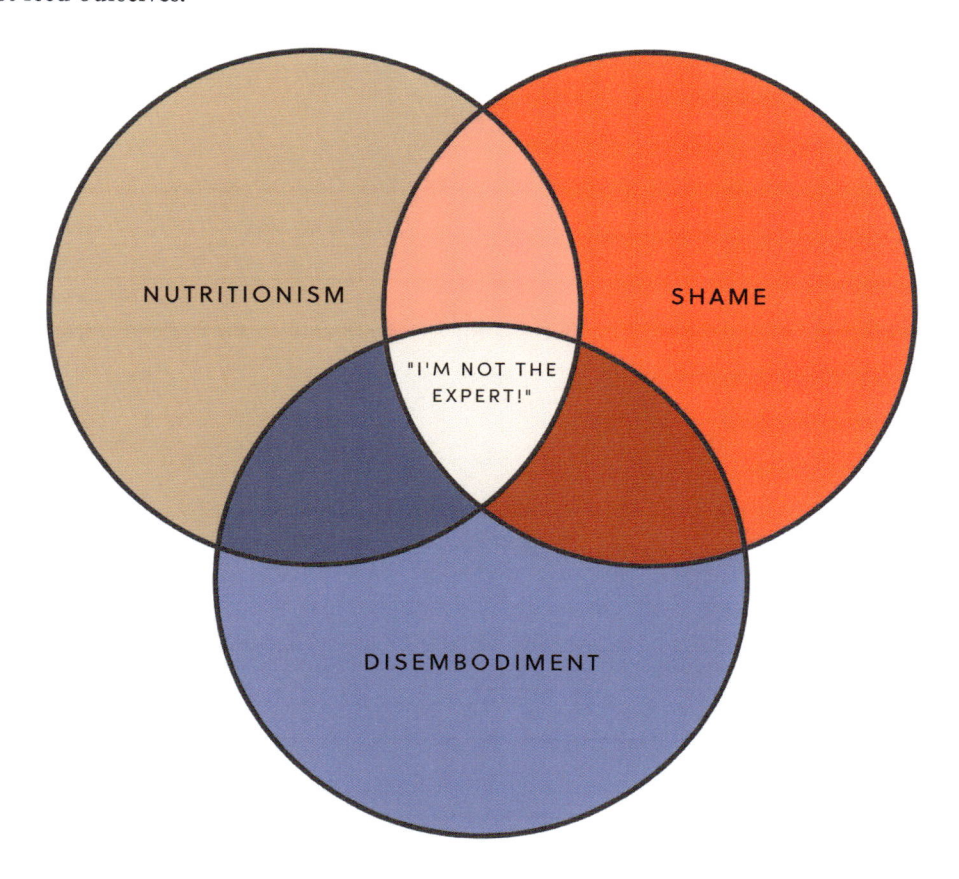

NUTRITIONISM

SHAME

"I'M NOT THE EXPERT!"

DISEMBODIMENT

SHAME

We live in a culture obsessed with shaming people about their bodies and their food choices. Our collective shame fuels a cultural obsession with having the "right," "good," or "perfect" body, and eating the "right," "good," or "perfect" way. When you're working harder to get food "right," than to eat what sounds, feels, and tastes good, being the expert is nearly impossible. Every time we challenge the voices that say, "You're doing it wrong. You're bad," or "You're never going to be thin unless you eat like _____," we're taking another step in the direction of freedom and healing.

DISEMBODIMENT

Most of us live in our heads, and as far away from our bodies and their sensations as we can get. Women in particular have experienced centuries of violence, judgment, objectification, and devaluation of their bodies, which makes living in them and trusting their wisdom challenging. If we don't live in our bodies, it's hard to embrace our role as the food expert, but if we practice listening to our physical cues, we will move towards living an embodied life.

NUTRITIONISM

Nutritionism is an ideology that believes that food's individual nutrients are what give it value, and that the only point of eating is for health. This is perhaps the most important idea in this week's lesson so I've also included an excerpt from Michael Pollan's New York Times piece, "Unhappy Meals[1]." I highly recommend that you read the full article to understand the extent that the "natural food" industry manipulates how we eat.

THE RISE OF NUTRITIONISM

The first thing to understand about nutritionism — I first encountered the term in the work of an Australian sociologist of science named Gyorgy Scrinis — is that it is not quite the same as nutrition. As the "ism" suggests, it is not a scientific subject but an ideology. Ideologies are ways of organizing large swaths of life and experience under a set of shared but unexamined assumptions. This quality makes an ideology particularly hard to see, at least while it's exerting its hold on your culture. A reigning ideology is a little like the weather, all pervasive and virtually inescapable. Still, we can try.

In the case of nutritionism, the widely shared but unexamined assumption is that the key to understanding food is indeed the nutrient. From this basic premise flow several others. Since nutrients, as compared with foods, are invisible and therefore slightly mysterious, it falls to the scientists (and to the journalists through whom the scientists speak) to explain the hidden reality of foods to us. To enter a world in which you dine on unseen nutrients, you need lots of expert help.

I can recall shouting righteously at my eating disorder therapist "Why would anyone ever eat an Oreo?!" She smiled and replied "For two reasons. One, they are delicious and that is reason enough. Two, Oreos, Snickers, and all quick-burning foods are great when you're needing a quick blood sugar boost." I didn't have a comeback for her but still clung to my nutritionist dogma so certain that the "right" way to eat was for physical health only.

Oh how confused I was all those years ago. Confused and hungry.

MORE THAN THE SUM OF ITS PARTS

Thousands of years of civilization have taught us that food is more than the nutrients that fuel our physical body. Food is ritual and connection, community and pleasure, medicine and tradition, celebration and culture. Food is sacred. Food is fun. Food is a means for expressing love, gratitude, care, and creativity. Holding this more holistic view of food doesn't threaten our health; it enhances it.

It is only in recent history that food has become mechanical, a form of punishment, something we can't trust ourselves around, and a means for determining one's worth. We've all experienced how this distortion of food's emotional, cultural and spiritual role in our life can lead to insanity.

We don't have to play this game anymore. We can say, "No, thank you," to the latest food fads, to diets that masquerade as healthy eating, and to well-meaning family members with nutrition dogma to share. We can say, "No, thank you," to dualistic thinking, rules, shame, lists of calories, and "allowed" foods. We can say, "No, thank you," to the worship of icons of food purity, and to the illusion that weight loss and being thin will sate what we're really hungry for: connection, love, acceptance, joy, meaning, service, creativity, and feeling good inside our body.

The world is filled with food and health "experts" and a general hysteria about what we put into our mouths. I'm not saying that the nutrients in food don't support our health; they absolutely do. I am saying that the fear and obsession that "experts" promote is dangerous. Your body is ready and willing to give you feedback about what food it likes and doesn't like. You are the expert of your own body. And with that responsibility comes a whole lot more freedom.

1 http://www.nytimes.com/2007/01/28/magazine/28nutritionism.t.html

WEEK SIX

REFLECTIONS ON EATING FREELY

Do I believe there are 'good' foods and 'bad' foods? Are there foods I don't allow myself to eat? Are there foods I don't enjoy that I make myself eat?

Are there any other food rules I try to follow (i.e. not eating after a certain time, no snacking, etc.)? If so...

When it comes to food, what tends to work for my body? What does my body tend to like? (type of food, time of day, quantity) How certain am I that this is based on feedback from my body and not a mental idea of what my body 'should' or 'shouldn't' eat? *Note: It's okay if you don't yet know what your body likes.*

If there were no labels of 'good/healthy' foods or 'bad/unhealthy' foods and I only had to rely on my tastebuds and bodily sensations my eating would probably look like:

Tracy Brown, an Intuitive Eating nutritionist, is now available in the Facebook group and on this week's live calls to answer any of my nutrition-focused questions. I want to remember to ask her:

Other than food, what do you think you're truly hungry for in your life?

INTUITIVE EATING QUESTIONS / CHAPTER EIGHT

In Chapter Eight, which line or passage was the most powerful? Transcribe here:

Did this week's reading assignment leave you with any questions?

WEEK SIX

CHALLENGE FOR EATING FREELY

One of your challenges this week is to purge your life of the things that interfere with your path to becoming a Well-fed Woman. This includes:

- *Books or cookbooks that promote a dieting, pro-weightloss mentality*

- *Cancel subscriptions to magazines that celebrate thinness and dieting (if you want to replace those magazine subscriptions have a look at: anthology, taproot, kinfolk, gather, or uppercase.)*

- *Unfollow people on social media that either contribute to the nutrition-obsession frenzy or promote a pro-weightloss agenda. These include: dr. Oz, jillian michaels, the biggest loser, weight watchers, and the like. This also includes people heavily focused on cleanses, raw diets, paleo diets, etc.*

- *If you haven't already, get rid of your scale and any kitchen gadgets (food scales, etc.) That are left over from your dieting days.*

- *Purge your pantry of any dieting foods that you don't enjoy eating that are leftover from days of deprivation.*

- *Optional: share a photo in the facebook group of all that you're letting go of.*

THE EATING FREELY EXPERIMENT

STEP ONE: COMPLETE THESE SENTENCES:

1. A food I love that I don't really allow myself to eat freely and enjoy is _____
2. I imagine that if I was totally free to eat [insert food you identified] I would eat [insert quantity].

STEP TWO: EAT!

1. Go out and procure [insert food] in the exact quantity (or more) you identified above.
2. When you're hungry, sit in a comfortable place and eat this food.
3. Do this without any distractions (no TV, no radio, no dining companions).
4. Simply eat and don't stop until it stops being a pleasurable experience and you're satiated.

As you eat, notice what you like about what you're eating. Notice if any strong thoughts or feelings arise. Notice if there is any fear present. Just be curious and notice while you enjoy your food.

5. You can go back for more when you're hungry again.

If you want to deepen your experience of this exercise you can try what the authors do at the bottom of page 108 where they provide an example of an eating experience broken out by the different internal voices. To try this, see what each has to say within you as you eat:
Food Police:

1. NUTRITION INFORMANT:

2. DIET REBEL:

WEEK SIX

3. FOOD ANTHROPOLOGIST:

4. NUTRITION ALLY:

5. NURTURER:

6. INTUITIVE EATER:

Reflect on your experience with this experiment: Copy and cut out the sign below and post it somewhere you can see it to remind you.

> I am the expert on my body.
>
> I choose to feed myself out of love, care and respect.
>
> Normal eating is flexible and pleasurable.
>
> Each day I recommit to the choices that free me.

WEEK SIX

EXPERT INTERVIEWEE

Dana Sturtevant & Hilary Kinavey

Dana Sturtevant, MS, RD, is a trainer, mentor, Kripalu Yoga teacher, and dietitian specializing in Health at Every Size® and intuitive eating. She is the cofounder of Be Nourished, a revolutionary business helping people heal body dissatisfaction and reclaim body trust. Dana loves incorporating mindfulness and self-compassion practices into her work. A member of the International Motivational Interviewing Network of Trainers, Dana has facilitated more than 300 workshops throughout the United States for health care providers looking to enhance their skills in behavior-change counseling. Her work has been featured in the Huffington Post.

Hilary Kinavey, MS, LPC, is a licensed professional counselor and co-founder of Be Nourished, LLC. Her work encourages movement toward a compassionate model of radical self-care to heal body shame and patterns of chronic dieting and disordered eating. She is the co-creator of Body Trust™ Wellness, a Certified Daring Way™ facilitator, and a transformational workshop leader. Hilary is a popular speaker on topics such as Health at Every Size®, intuitive eating, and body respect in health care communities, and a regular contributor to the Huffington Post.

Visit *benourished.org* to learn more about Dana and Hilary's work.

NOTES

Want more?

Then check out these related posts that Rachel has written.

A TIME FOR EVERYTHING
http://goo.gl/H9sSLk

A SWEET MIDDLE PATH
http://goo.gl/RtePct

TASTE TEST
http://goo.gl/ns2O8J

THE DANGER OF GREEN JUICES
http://goo.gl/7iF7BG

WEEK SIX

NOTES

DAILY PRACTICE CHECKLIST

GENERAL *FEAST* SKILLS	S 9/4	M 9/5	T 9/6	W 9/7	Th 9/8	F 9/9	Sa 9/10
Meditated (on own or with recording)							
Read Feast Material							
Wrote responses to reflection questions							
Listened to expert interview/live call							
Reached out to the group for support							
Meditated (on own or with recording)							
Meditated (on own or with recording)							

SELF-COMPASSION SKILLS	S 9/4	M 9/5	T 9/6	W 9/7	Th 9/8	F 9/9	Sa 9/10
Spoke kindly to myself							
Acted self-compassionately toward myself							

WEEK SIX

CARE FOR SENSITIVE SOUL SKILLS	S 9/4	M 9/5	T 9/6	W 9/7	Th 9/8	F 9/9	Sa 9/10
Attempted to mangage my sensory input							
Advocated for my HSP needs							
Celebrated/observed my HSP strengths							

EFFECTIVE EMOTIONAL COPING SKILLS	S 9/4	M 9/5	T 9/6	W 9/7	Th 9/8	F 9/9	Sa 9/10
Paused!							
RAIN (recognize, allow, investigate, natural awareness)							
Made a concious choice to distract							
Urge surfed							
Reached out to the group for support							
Did cost/benefit analysis							
Went in slo-mo							

HUNGER/FULLNESS SKILLS	S 9/4	M 9/5	T 9/6	W 9/7	Th 9/8	F 9/9	Sa 9/10
Recognized bodily cues re: hunger/fullness							
Honored bodily cues re: hunger/fullness							
Used the hunger-fullness scale							
Ate when I was hungry (before starving)							
Stopped when I was satisfied (before stuffed)							

EATING FREELY SKILLS	S 9/4	M 9/5	T 9/6	W 9/7	Th 9/8	F 9/9	Sa 9/10
Turned away from nutrition noise and toward my inner wisdom							
Made food choices for reasons beyond nutrition or health							
Made choices, rather than deferred to 'shoulds' or 'shouldnt's'							
Challenged the good/bad label I once placed on food(s)							

WEEK SEVEN

Pleasure & Satisfaction

AT THE TABLE

One of the most startling discoveries I've made on my own healing path is that pleasure is not a bad thing.

Gasp!

Not only is pleasure not bad; we don't need to stop ourselves from having it.

Gasp!

We are not bad for indulging in pleasure.

Gasp!

How miraculous to discover that my body, our bodies, have built in pleasure sensors that tell us when we need more, and when we've had enough.

> **Reminder!**
>
> **This week please read Chapter Ten in *Intuitive Eating*.**

In fact, pleasure is one of our best allies in figuring out what we're hungry for. Think of it like a north star, all we need to do is find it and walk towards it.

Unfortunately, it can take a while to trust that pleasure is our friend.

Centuries of human culture and religion have taught us that pleasure is not to be trusted and being indulgent can be anything from selfish to dangerous. These deeply rooted beliefs, which can often be traced back to patriarchal societies, still hold strong today. All it takes is for us to watch an hour of television to witness the message that indulging in pleasure = guilt and shame.

Let's talk first about indulgence. Say it a few times and notice what happens in your body.

Indulgence.

Indulgence.

Indulgence.

Does it feel naughty to even say it?

The definition of, *indulge*, and this was a surprise to me, is to, "allow oneself to enjoy the pleasure of." *Pleasure* is defined as, "a feeling of happy satisfaction and enjoyment." Now if that doesn't sound like good old healthy human behavior, I don't know what is.

Let that soak in for a moment.

When you're indulging, you're simply allowing yourself to enjoy the pleasure of something. It might be a doughnut. It might be a pedicure. It might be taking off from work early to enjoy a spring day.

It's long past time that we reclaim pleasure and indulgence from the puritanical police.

PLEASURE FEARS

Experiencing pleasure is not the same thing as numbing out, or distraction. When we numb out, we can experience a lessening of discomfort, but chances are, we aren't experiencing true pleasure. Pleasure is not just the absence of pain.

I'm sure some of you are wondering, "Can't you indulge too much? Isn't there such a thing as too much pleasure? If I let myself eat whatever and however much brings me pleasure, will I ever stop eating?"

The short answer is no, you can't indulge too much. If you let yourself use pleasure as your guide, you won't eat forever.

The long answer is a bit more nuanced.

The two steps we need to take to add true pleasure back into our lives are to pay attention and to receive.

Have you ever sat down to eat and finished before you even tasted a bite? That is a pleasure-free eating experience. If you are physically present for pleasure, but not paying attention to it, not soaking it up, it might as well not have happened at all.

OPENING UP TO PLEASURE

Just like a camera has an aperture that controls how much light it lets in, we each have an internal aperture of sorts that controls how much pleasure we allow ourselves to experience. For many of us, our aperture is quite narrow because we've been conditioned to be wary of pleasure and to indulge minimally.

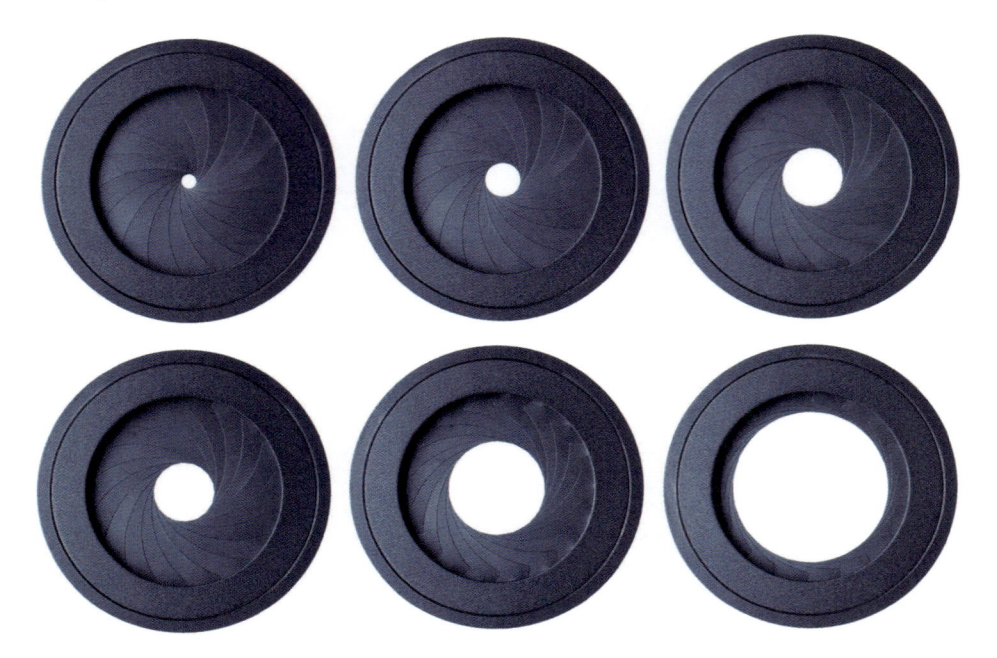

So how do we begin to open our pleasure aperture?

Bit by bit.

By paying attention when we experience it.

By taking in pleasure when it is available, so that it can actually fill us up.

By using our whole body, not just our brain, to determine when to keeping going, and when to stop.

By trusting ourselves.

By making integrated decisions.

Our old way of thinking was black and white, and enforced strict rules that someone else created. Our new way of thinking embraces the many nuances of gray, and the empowered choices we make each moment.

For example, I might get a lot of pleasure from eating a bowl of coffee ice cream when I'm hungry before going to bed. I love the taste of coffee ice cream, and ice cream is very satisfying when I'm hungry. Experience has taught me that if I eat coffee ice cream before bed, I will have a hard time sleeping because I'm very sensitive to caffeine.

These thoughts and feelings don't mean I should, or shouldn't eat the ice cream; it just means that there are several factors I can weigh in order to make an integrated decision. Presented with this same scenario multiple times, I might make a different choice each time depending on what's important to me in a given moment. This is what being an empowered eater looks like.

Opening our pleasure aperture is not about green lighting everything that tastes good all the time; it is about valuing pleasure as one part of normal, healthy eating.

WHY PLEASURE IS IMPORTANT

Even if we eat enough calorically, if we haven't eaten what we truly want to eat, or what brings us pleasure, it's very difficult to feel full. Pleasure is fundamental for achieving fullness, and honoring our fullness is essential to having a peaceful relationship with food.

Opening up to pleasure may feel uncomfortable, especially if you've been told all your life that pleasure is bad, and that you need to shy away from it at the table, or other places in your life. I invite you to dip your toe into pleasure slowly. Be open to what pleasure can do for you on your healing path.

Pleasure is a food group. Make sure you're getting enough daily servings.

WEEK SEVEN

REFLECTIONS ON PLEASURE AND SATISFACTION

Do a mind-map for the word pleasure. What words, thoughts, fears, dreams, concepts, questions, and memories come to mind when you think of pleasure? Write them out by drawing branches off of the central 'pleasure' hub.

Pleasure

What do you notice about your pleasure mind map? What's your 'story' about pleasure?

What happens when you deny a food craving or stop yourself from finishing something you still want to eat?

What happens when you eat food that is "good for you" but isn't all that yummy?

Make a list here of all things you can think of, food and otherwise, that give you a lot of pleasure:

Notice how many of these you experience regularly. Notice which of your senses (or plus your heart/spirit) each of these is connected to.

Other than food, what do you think you're truly hungry for in your life?

WEEK SEVEN

INTUITIVE EATING QUESTIONS / CHAPTER TEN

In Chapter 10, which line or passage was the most powerful? Transcribe here:

Did this week's reading assignment leave you with any questions?

PLEASURE AND SATISFACTION CHALLENGES

While it's not always possible, this week your challenge is eat only what you really enjoy eating AND to pay attention to/receive the pleasure in these experiences of eating. We want you to be able to say at the end of the day that everything you ate was totally delicious.

Have a go and reflect on your experience and what this challenge brings up for you here:

Your second challenge this week is to seek out a peak, or near peak, pleasure experience once this week. If we rank pleasure on a 1-10 scale with 10 being 'peak pleasure experience' see if you can have one of those at least three times this week. Don't be perfectionistic about this. Any increased pleasure is to be celebrated. This can food-based pleasure but you're encouraged to include other pleasure sources as well.

Reflect on your experience here:

WEEK SEVEN

EXPERT INTERVIEWEE

Carmen Cool

Carmen Cool MA, LPC is a psychotherapist in private practice in Boulder, Colorado. She is also a certified Hakomi therapist, using a body-centered, mindfulness-based approach to eating and weight concerns. As founder of the former Boulder Youth Body Alliance in 2004, she has championed youth to raise their voice and create new cultural norms around body image. She was named "Most Inspiring Individual" in Boulder County and won the Excellence in Eating Disorder Advocacy Award in Washington DC. She currently serves as the president for the Association of Size Diversity and Health (ASDAH). Visit *carmencool.com* for additional information about Carmen and her work as a psychotherapist, educator, and activist.

NOTES

Want more?

Then check out these related posts that Rachel has written.

CAROLYN'S LOVELY FREEING EATING GUIDE
http://goo.gl/lKNPEv

P IS FOR PLEASURE
http://goo.gl/Wyox34

PLEASUARY
http://goo.gl/dHvxcq

WEEK SEVEN

NOTES

NOTES

WEEK SEVEN

DAILY PRACTICE CHECKLIST

GENERAL *FEAST* SKILLS	S 9/11	M 9/12	T 9/13	W 9/14	Th 9/15	F 9/16	Sa 9/17
Meditated (on own or with recording)							
Read Feast Material							
Wrote responses to reflection questions							
Listened to expert interview/live call							
Reached out to the group for support							
Meditated (on own or with recording)							
Meditated (on own or with recording)							

SELF-COMPASSION SKILLS	S 9/11	M 9/12	T 9/13	W 9/14	Th 9/15	F 9/16	Sa 9/17
Spoke kindly to myself							
Acted self-compassionately toward myself							

CARE FOR SENSITIVE SOUL SKILLS	S 9/11	M 9/12	T 9/13	W 9/14	Th 9/15	F 9/16	Sa 9/17
Attempted to mangage my sensory input							
Advocated for my HSP needs							
Celebrated/observed my HSP strengths							

EFFECTIVE EMOTIONAL COPING SKILLS	S 9/11	M 9/12	T 9/13	W 9/14	Th 9/15	F 9/16	Sa 9/17
Paused!							
RAIN (recognize, allow, investigate, natural awareness)							
Made a concious choice to distract							
Urge surfed							
Reached out to the group for support							
Did cost/benefit analysis							
Went in slo-mo							

WEEK SEVEN

HUNGER/FULLNESS SKILLS	S 9/11	M 9/12	T 9/13	W 9/14	Th 9/15	F 9/16	Sa 9/17
Recognized bodily cues re: hunger/fullness							
Honored bodily cues re: hunger/fullness							
Used the hunger-fullness scale							
Ate when I was hungry (before starving)							
Stopped when I was satisfied (before stuffed)							

EATING FREELY SKILLS	S 9/11	M 9/12	T 9/13	W 3/16	Th 9/15	F 9/16	Sa 9/17
Turned away from nutrition noise and toward my inner wisdom							
Made food choices for reasons beyond nutrition or health							
Made choices, rather than deferred to 'shoulds' or 'shouldnt's'							
Challenged the good/bad label I once placed on food(s)							

PLEASURE & SATISFACTION SKILLS	S 9/11	M 9/12	T 9/13	W 9/14	Th 9/15	F 9/16	Sa 9/17
I chose to do/eat/receive something because it would give me pleasure							
I chose to do/eat/receive for pleasure without having to earn it or feel guilty							
I paid attention what I was doing/eating/ receiving so as to maximize my pleasure							
I experienced the connection between pleasurable eating and feeling physically satisfied/full							

WEEK EIGHT

Joyful Movement

AT THE TABLE

As a child, my body felt like a liability.

I felt uncoordinated, unfit, inflexible, and weak.

Physical education class nearly always left me in hysterics. The pressure to perform, catch (or worse, dodge) the ball, run a mile, or touch my toes induced panic.

My mother says that when she asked me if I wanted to join a sports team, I firmly replied, "No." I don't recall saying that, and wish she, or another adult, had been more encouraging of me in that direction. Perhaps then I would have developed a functional relationship with my body, one that was about what it could do, and less about how it looked, or what it couldn't do.

Alas, my childhood and adolescent years were spent longing for the American fitness ideal (e.g. "rockin' abs") and feeling shame that I was nowhere near achieving it. In the seventh grade, I'd come home from school, stand naked in front of my full-length mirror, and lament not my body size, but my general lack of muscle tone.

When I started college, I thought I'd find salvation at the campus fitness center, but my panic attacks followed me there too. I felt such intense shame and judgment working out amidst the varsity athletes that retreating to my dorm room, and as far away from physical pursuits as possible, felt like the only option.

At 18 years old, I still had no idea that moving my body could feel good, or that a reason to move my body could be for pleasure. I'd been on the planet for nearly two decades, and this most basic of human truths had escaped me. At this point, the only thing I knew, or thought I knew, was that fit bodies were preferred to flabby bodies, and that no pain, meant no gain.

During my junior year, after a stint living abroad in Italy, I managed to get myself to the campus gym regularly. I did so by going at the crack of dawn and mustering a fierce, compulsive energy that quickly evolved into fuel for anorexia. By 21 or 22, my compulsive exercise regime had rendered me bedridden with a hip that ached 24/7. It appeared that I could not outrun, or under eat my way to peace. I was going to have to sit still and deal with myself.

As I began to explore and heal my relationship to food, the lessons I learned at the table couldn't help but be applied to my life away from the table as well. If my body had the wisdom to tell me about what I was hungry for, when to eat, and when I was full, then it certainly had the wisdom to tell me how and when I wanted to move.

If my body wasn't the enemy when it came to food, then it couldn't be the enemy when it came to movement. If I didn't need to punish myself at the table, then I certainly didn't need to punish myself at the gym. If I could trust my body to have a natural rhythm of hunger and fullness, then I could trust my body to have a natural rhythm of rest and movement, a rhythm I didn't need to control.

Suddenly everything started to click into place.

Healing my relationship to movement has, admittedly, taken a lot longer than healing my relationship to food. Coming home to joyful movement has required more patience and self-compassion. I also think that because I deeply associated exercise with punishment and pain, it took a long time for me to cultivate a movement practice that I associated with pleasure.

Oh, and that painful hip. It's not perfect, even today, over a decade later. I have had lots of physical therapy, and learned stretches and exercises that help, but I gave up the idea that my body was ever meant to run long ago. Truthfully, I'm so grateful my hip gave out on me. If it hadn't, I might still be trying to control my life with minutes spent on a treadmill. I think of my hip like the canary in the coal mine; it lets me know when something isn't right and when I'm not listening.

> ## Reminder!
> This week please read Chapters Twelve and Thirteen in *Intuitive Eating*.

My hip injury also pushed me to discover swimming and yoga, two practices I doubt I'd ever have discovered if I wasn't in so much pain. The amazing thing to me is that my compulsive tendencies didn't follow me into the lap lane or onto the mat. From my first swimming lesson (which I totally recommend adults take), I knew that I wasn't going to count laps, minutes, calories or anything else. I even heard my inner compassionate voice tell me, "The water takes you just as you are." This has become my movement mantra through the years, even in the yoga studio, where I say to myself, "The mat takes me just as I am."

As we head into our week focused on joyful movement, know that the information in this chapter is here to support your being kind to yourself, connecting deeper with your body, and having more ease. If at any point you feel like joyful movement is just another "should," drop it. Don't ever move because you "should," move because your body wants it, it feels good, and because doing so feels like a tender act of love.

Below are 11 things I know about joyful movement and breaking through the impediments that keep us from moving:

1. **THE BODY WANTS TO MOVE.**

    All bodies want to move. Not all the time and not in all ways, but all bodies want to move.

2. **WE OFTEN NEED AN ALLY.**

    Ask a friend, movement therapist, yoga teacher, or any other compassionate movement professional to support your creating a movement practice that is joy-centered rather than weight loss centered. A little personal suggestion: When I go to a new yoga, or Pilates class, I often write a note on a 3 x 5 card introducing myself and explaining that I'm not interested in weight loss or shaping my body, only in listening to my body and feeling good. I slip it to the teacher before class starts. This is just one way I can advocate for my body and find movement allies in the world.

3. WE HAVE TO WORK THROUGH OLD STORIES THAT AREN'T TRUE.

So much of the path to becoming a well-fed woman is about noticing the stories that have run amok in our heads. Stories like "I'm weak," "I'm lazy," "I can't exercise without thinking about calories," or "If it's not an intense workout it doesn't count." All of these thoughts come from the same critical, harsh place: our ego. Although these kinds of stories are trying to keep us safe, they aren't true and ultimately don't support us. The good news is we can learn to hear them without letting them run the show. We can learn to write a new, more honest and friendly story.

4. PAIN IS NOT A DEAD END.

My body has hurt most of my life. I've had a host of orthopedic ailments that don't typically present until much later in life. I've been injured. I've been out of alignment. One of my legs is longer than the other and my spine is not straight. Despite all of this, I've learned that pain is not a dead end when it comes to movement. Pain means we may have to move more mindfully, and in a way that is friendlier to our body. Pain means we may have to take time to heal and get help with healing. Pain means we might have a different set of requirements when it comes to movement than someone in a sturdier body, but pain is not a dead end.

5. LACK OF SKILL IS TEMPORARY.

We may never have learned how to swim, or have the faintest idea how to play softball, or do a yoga pose. We might long to ride a bike, belly dance, or go skiing, but lack of know-how stops us. All of this can change. If there is a movement style that you want to try, but don't know how, take a lesson, have a friend teach you, watch a YouTube video, or if it's not too dangerous, be willing to awkwardly just try it. It's never too late to learn a new way to move if it's what your body is asking for. Be a beginner with pride!

6. IT ALL COUNTS.

I used to think that if I didn't break a sweat or if I moved for less than thirty minutes, it didn't count. It all counts. If you move, it counts. Sometimes our body wants to writhe slowly like molasses spreading across our bedroom floor. Sometimes it wants to twirl like a whirling dervish. Sometimes our body wants to lift heavy things or climb steep mountains, and on other days it wants to stroll to the mailbox and get back into bed. Don't let dualistic thinking rob you of small acts of joyful movement. It all counts.

7. THIS IS JUST ANOTHER NATURAL CYCLE.

Just like waking and sleeping, eating and digesting, bleeding and ovulating, we all have natural cycles of movement and rest. Each of these cycles gives us physical cues that tell us what is needed during that part of the cycle. It may have been a long time since we've heard or listened to these cues, but they are still there saying, "Let's move!" or "Let's rest!" The more we practice honoring our individual cycles, the more harmony we'll bring to our body.

8. **JOYFUL MOVEMENT IS ENTIRELY ABOUT THE "WHY."**

   There is nothing inherently alarming about running a marathon, or benign about lying on a couch all weekend. It's all about the "why." Are we making a choice because we're afraid, we want to lose weight, or we're punishing ourselves for eating dessert? Are we making a choice because it's what our body is asking for, it brings us pleasure, or because it's just plain old fun? When it comes to movement, we have to ask ourselves why we're doing, or not doing something, and then make choices from a place of kindness.

9. **TASTE THE RAINBOW.**

   There are an infinite number of ways to move our bodies and all bodies have preferences for which type of movement feels best to them. Finding a joyful movement practice that suits us is about being willing to try a wide range of movement styles. Just as we can learn what foods we like to eat by trying a range of flavors (salty, sweet, sour, bitter, umami), we can also try different kinds of movement (high intensity, low intensity, individual, group, indoor, outdoor, with music, in silence, casual, competitive).

10. **AWKWARDNESS IS THE NAME OF THE GAME (IN THE BEGINNING).**

    I have often felt self-conscious and anxious attempting to move my body. I feared what others would think of me. I would obsess about having the right workout clothes, and dread being the student who couldn't keep up, or who had two left feet. These fears still rear their head from time to time, but now when I start a new movement practice, I remind myself that most of us feel awkward when we begin something. It's a nearly universal experience, and more importantly, a temporary one.

11. **LETHARGY AND FATIGUE ARE TWO DIFFERENT THINGS.**

    I learned this from my friend, and author of *Zen Under Fire*, Marianne Elliot[1]. She taught me that we often confuse the two. Lethargy is when we're tired, and movement makes us feel better and more energized. Fatigue is when we're tired and movement makes us feel exhausted. This distinction helps me to better understand the messages around movement that my body sends me.

This week, more than any of the previous weeks, is about meeting yourself where you are. It's about tiny, consistent visits with your body to metaphorically, "open the windows and let the sunshine in." Only you and your body know what you need. Take advantage of the *Feast* community and join in by moving your body in a joyful way!

---

1 http://marianne-elliott.com

WEEK EIGHT

REFLECTIONS ON JOYFUL MOVEMENT

What's your history with body movement or exercise?

What's your current 'story' about moving your body? Do you have any fears about body movement that might be impeding a joyful movement practice?

What kind of movement does your body dislike? What time of day does it most enjoy moving?

What kind of movement is your body asking for at this moment in your life? How often is it asking to
move?

Other than food, what do you think you're truly hungry for in your life?

INTUITIVE EATING QUESTIONS / CHAPTER TWELVE AND THIRTEEN

In Chapter 12, which line or passage was the most powerful? Transcribe here:

In Chapter 13, which line or passage was the most powerful? Transcribe here:

Did this week's reading assignment leave you with any questions?

WEEK EIGHT

CHALLENGES FOR JOYFUL MOVEMENT

Your body wants to move. It might want to move fast or slow. It might want to move indoors or outdoors. It might want to move with others or alone. It might not know yet how it wants to move, but it wants to move. *Every body wants to move.*

Your challenge this week is to begin a daily movement practice. It doesn't have to take a lot of time, though it can if that's what you're craving and can afford. Your challenge is simply to move your body joyfully once a day. Think of a joyful movement as something that if I asked your body "How was that?" it would reply "That was really pleasurable." or "That felt amazing." or "I loved that." It all counts. Five minutes of stretching on your bedroom floor counts just as much as a day-long hike. Ask your body "What would feel good?"

A SHORT LIST OF IDEAS FOR JOYFUL MOVEMENT

- *Drop into a movement class (yoga, nia, aqua aerobics, etc.)*
- *Dance at home or go out dancing*
- *Go for a stroll in your neighborhood*
- *Take a nature walk or hike*
- *Take a photo walk and try to snap 10 pics of things that are beautiful or of every color of the rainbow.*
- *Ask a friend to play catch, tennis, basketball, or kickball with you.*
- *Throwback to your childhood with hula hoops, jump ropes, hokey pokey, or hop scotch*
- *Try a guided yoga practice at home (check out www.curvyyoga.com)*
- *Get out into the yard and do some gardening*
- *Wiggle. Just wiggle. Wiggle how ever your body wants to wiggle*

A FEW TIPS FOR CULTIVATING A JOYFUL MOVEMENT PRACTICE

1. *Joyful movement is not about what you 'should' do it's about what you want to do. We're told a lot of things about exercise and what's ideal, for now, throw all that out and just listen inward to what would, or could, delight your body.*

2. *This is an experiment. Just like ordering a new item off a menu, you won't know if you like it until you try it. Be open to trying new things and be open to liking, or not liking, how they feel.*

3. *Consider the structure or support that might help you. Such as: scheduling your movement time in your calendar, making a date to move with a friend, getting shoes or clothing that feel really good to move in, planning to move during the time of day that works for you.*

4. *If you feel resistance, consider if you might just be afraid (of doing it wrong, of judging/feeling your current body as it is, etc.). If this is the case, try moving anyways, with as little judgment as possible. Just showing the part of you that's scared that this movement is about pleasure not about pain or pressure.*

WEEK EIGHT

EXPERT INTERVIEWEE

Anna Guest-Jelley

Anna Guest-Jelley is founder and CEO (Curvy Executive Officer) at Curvy Yoga, a training and inspiration portal offering classes, workshops, teacher trainings, retreats, a virtual yoga studio and lots of love and support to people of every shape and size — all over the world.

Anna is a writer, teacher and lifelong champion for women's empowerment and body acceptance. Co-editor of *Yoga and Body Image: 25 Personal Stories About Beauty, Bravery & Loving Your Body*, Anna has been featured online and in print at *The New York Times, The Washington Post, xoJane, The Daily Love, MariaShriver.com, US News & World Report, Southern Living, Vogue Italia, Yoga International, Yoga Journal* and more. Learn more about Anna and Curvy Yoga at *CurvyYoga.com*

EXPERT INTERVIEWEE

Rachel Marcus

Rachel Marcus is a Masters student in Holistic Health Education and an ACE Certified Personal Trainer with Rachel Marcus Personal Training in Oakland, CA. She works with people one-on-one and in groups to enjoy exercise and movement in a weight-neutral, supportive, inclusive, body-positive environment. She believes in the power of movement as a path to self-love and gaining a deeper awareness of our bodies. She leads workshops on Health at Every Size and joyful movement in various places in the Bay Area. You can find out more at *rmarcusfitness.com*.

WEEK EIGHT

NOTES

NOTES

WEEK EIGHT

NOTES

DAILY PRACTICE CHECKLIST

GENERAL *FEAST* SKILLS	S 9/18	M 9/19	T 9/20	W 9/21	Th 9/22	F 9/23	Sa 9/24
Meditated (on own or with recording)							
Read Feast Material							
Wrote responses to reflection questions							
Listened to expert interview/live call							
Reached out to the group for support							
Meditated (on own or with recording)							
Meditated (on own or with recording)							

SELF-COMPASSION SKILLS	S 9/18	M 9/19	T 9/20	W 9/21	Th 9/22	F 9/23	Sa 9/24
Spoke kindly to myself							
Acted self-compassionately toward myself							

WEEK EIGHT

CARE FOR SENSITIVE SOUL SKILLS	S 9/18	M 9/19	T 9/20	W 9/21	Th 9/22	F 9/23	Sa 9/24
Attempted to mangage my sensory input							
Advocated for my HSP needs							
Celebrated/observed my HSP strengths							

EFFECTIVE EMOTIONAL COPING SKILLS	S 9/18	M 9/19	T 9/20	W 9/21	Th 9/22	F 9/23	Sa 9/24
Paused!							
RAIN (recognize, allow, investigate, natural awareness)							
Made a concious choice to distract							
Urge surfed							
Reached out to the group for support							
Did cost/benefit analysis							
Went in slo-mo							

HUNGER/FULLNESS SKILLS	S 9/18	M 9/19	T 9/20	W 9/21	Th 9/22	F 9/23	Sa 9/24
Recognized bodily cues re: hunger/fullness							
Honored bodily cues re: hunger/fullness							
Used the hunger-fullness scale							
Ate when I was hungry (before starving)							
Stopped when I was satisfied (before stuffed)							

EATING FREELY SKILLS	S 9/18	M 9/19	T 9/20	W 9/21	Th 9/22	F 9/23	Sa 9/24
Turned away from nutrition noise and toward my inner wisdom							
Made food choices for reasons beyond nutrition or health							
Made choices, rather than deferred to 'shoulds' or 'shouldnt's'							
Challenged the good/bad label I once placed on food(s)							

WEEK EIGHT

PLEASURE & SATISFACTION SKILLS	S 9/18	M 9/19	T 9/20	W 9/21	Th 9/22	F 9/23	Sa 9/24
I chose to do/eat/receive something because it would give me pleasure							
I chose to do/eat/receive for pleasure without having to earn it or feel guilty							
I paid attention what I was doing/eating/receiving so as to maximize my pleasure							
I experienced the connection between pleasurable eating and feeling physically satisfied/full							

JOYFUL MOVEMENT SKILLS	S 9/18	M 9/19	T 9/20	W 9/21	Th 9/22	F 9/23	Sa 9/24
I moved my body in some way that felt good/joyful/pleasurable to my body							
I rested my body when it requested rest							
I released old thoughts of exercising for punishment or as a means to earn the right to eat more							
I released self-judgement about what others might think of my body when I'm joyfully moving							

WEEK NINE

Integration Week

―――

AT THE TABLE

WEEK NINE

It only takes a reminder to breathe, a moment to be still, and just like that, something in me settles, softens, makes space for imperfection. The harsh voice of judgment drops to a whisper and I remember again that life isn't a relay race; that we will all cross the finish line; that waking up to life is what we were born for. As many times as I forget, catch myself charging forward without even knowing where I'm going, that many times I can make the choice to stop, to breathe, and be, and walk slowly into the mystery.

DANNA FAULDS

Enjoy your integration week! Reflect. Rest. Practice. Savor.

xo

Rachel

NOTES

WEEK NINE

NOTES

NOTES

WEEK TEN

Becoming a Well-fed Woman

Part I

LIVING A WELL-FED LIFE

As I walked the path of self-compassion and intuitive eating, my paradigm shift around living a well-fed life came naturally. This doesn't mean it's been easy to live a well-fed life, just that my awakening was.

As I began to understand that I wasn't broken, I was lovable, my body was wise, and that my food hungers could be trusted, it dawned on me: I COULDN'T HONOR MY FOOD HUNGERS WITHOUT HONORING ALL OF MY HUNGERS. Honoring all of our hungers is the basis for what I call "well-fed living."

To live a well-fed life is to be guided by four beliefs:

1. *All of our hungers are wise. They form the internal compass that points us toward what we need.*

2. *We are all equally worthy of being well-fed. No one is more or less worthy of having a well-fed life.*

3. *When we're well-fed, we can be fully engaged and effective in life. Feeding ourselves is an act of service.*

4. *A world full of well-fed people (especially women) is a better world.*

Although these beliefs may seem quite simple, they are also radical. As women in the modern world, we are given the message at home, at school, professionally and culturally to be quiet, small, and selfless, to not feed ourselves. These beliefs have been reinforced throughout history, in modern times in particular, when millions of dollars are spent on advertisements and entertainment with an anti-well-fed woman message.

Shaking off such an ingrained way of thinking and embracing the new well-fed woman paradigm can be a challenge. But if we remind ourselves every day that the old way of living as a "hungry woman" isn't sustainable, and hasn't taken us where we want to go, we can transform. If we are willing to shift our perspective, and approach our hungers as friends rather than foes, we will become well-fed women.

This is not a quick fix, a three-step process, a perfect science, or even a science at all. It's a new paradigm that allows us to make choices and take actions that make us feel alive and full. When we are our most alive and full selves, we are able to be of service in a healthy and effective way. And that's what the world needs.

It's a misconception to think that well-fed women are never hungry, have an easy breezy time feeding their hungers, and effortlessly identify their hungers.

Well-fed women get hungry because the natural cycle of taking in and expending what is life-giving doesn't end until we die. We consume what nourishes us (e.g. food, time in nature, creative projects) and then, after awhile, we get hungry again. This is natural. Well-fed women get hungry.

Well-fed women are not magicians. They can't just wave a wand upon realizing that they are hungry for healthy intimacy, or meaningful work, and conjure up a partner, or a new job offer. What well-fed women do is listen to their hungers, stay in relationship to them (rather than numbing, judging, or going down the "it's not possible" path), and slowly move in the direction of what feeds them.

Well-fed women also know that it's easy, and normal to sometimes lose touch with their hungers in this noisy world. They don't always hear the call from within for what they are hungry for. What well-fed women do differently is make a practice of consciously asking and listening for hunger cues. They do this with the belief that their hungers are wise and worthy of being fed.

7 BARRIERS TO BECOMING A WELL-FED WOMAN AND THEIR ANTIDOTES

BARRIER	ANTIDOTE
LACK OF SELF-COMPASSION	*You're not alone if you have a hard time with self-compassion. Start by having self-compassion for your struggle to have self-compassion. Keep trying. Practice loving-kindness meditation. Think less; actively love yourself more.*
"I'M LESS WORTHY OR MORE BROKEN THAN OTHERS."	*Commit to waking up from this omnipresent, ego-based illusion. Seek out a meditation practice that works for you. Address this myth with a therapist or coach.*
"I'M AFRAID OF BEING NEEDY OR SELFISH."	*Remember that feeding yourself is an act of service. Women who stay small don't contribute nearly as much as women who fill up! Feast! Do it for the rest of us.*
"I'M AFRAID OF THE PAIN OF WANTING, THE FEELING THAT HAPPENS BEFORE I'M FED."	*Yes, there is pain, but not feeding yourself is it's own kind of pain AND the more consistently we feed ourselves the less painful hunger becomes because our nervous system trusts that nourishment is on the way.*

BARRIER	ANTIDOTE
"I'M AFRAID THAT IT'S NOT POSSIBLE FOR ME TO FEED MY HUNGERS. I'M AFRAID THAT WHAT I WANT IS JUST TOO BIG, TOO MUCH, OR TOO FAR FETCHED."	*Well, this one is common. In fact, everyone feels this way. This is a self-protective mechanism. It is almost always possible when we get down to the core (or Primary hunger) of what we're seeking to feed ourselves our truest desire.*
"I KNOW WHAT I'M HUNGRY FOR BUT I HAVE NO CLUE HOW TO FEED IT."	*That's 100% OK. We have to start with the "what" before we get to the "how." In fact, we are often way too quick to jump to the how.*
"I DON'T LISTEN. I DON'T SET ASIDE FIVE MINUTES EVEN ONCE A WEEK TO TURN INWARD AND INQUIRE ABOUT MY HUNGERS."	*When you step fully onto the path of becoming a Well-fed Woman you commit yourself to regularly going inward to listen. It might not always be convenient or a fully developed practice at the start, and you won't always hear a clear answer, or even like what you hear, but you commit to listening.*

HOW DO I KNOW WHAT I'M HUNGRY FOR?

You listen. Yes, I know I've said this before, but it truly is the cornerstone to knowing your hungers.

You're listening for what would feel fulfilling. You're inquiring into what would make you feel more alive, full, at ease, and nourished. Ask yourself now.

One exercise I give to clients is to imagine a metaphorical buffet table. Everything you want is on that table (and we're not talking food here, though that can be there too). What do you want a big bowl of? What would you have served on a platter? This is just one way to begin to listen inward.

Another exercise I often give is to journal the answers to these two questions each night:

>   WHAT FED ME TODAY?
>   WHAT WILL FEED ME TOMORROW?

SEPARATING FEELING FROM FEEDING

The process of opening a dialogue with our hungers and inviting them to speak is so important that it needs to be treated as a stand-alone stage. What often happens is that because we can become stressed out by *how* we're going to fulfill our hunger, we don't let ourselves hear *what* our hunger is. We are so afraid that when we hear what we hunger for we'll have to do something about it, that we turn down the volume on our inner voice.

We don't need to do this.

When we give ourselves permission and space to name our hungers without worrying about how we will fulfill them, we can hear the answer to that favorite question, "What am I truly hungry for?" Without any pressure to act or solve the how, the truth can be revealed.

This week, give yourself space to listen to your hungers without drifting into your "fix-it" mind.

PRIMARY HUNGERS VS. SECONDARY HUNGERS

We have two kinds of hungers: primary and secondary.

Primary hungers are things that human beings have always hungered for and needed. They are general and universal, and are the source of our secondary hungers. Primary hungers are our true root desires. When they are satisfied, we feel satiated and at ease.

Below is a list of some of the primary hungers you might have at any given moment:

- ABUNDANCE
- ADORNMENT
- ADVENTURE
- AFFECTION
- BELONGING
- CARBOHYDRATES
- CHANGE
- CLARITY
- CLEANLINESS
- COMFORT
- CONNECTION TO COMMUNITY
- CONNECTION TO FAMILY
- CONNECTION TO NATURE
- CONNECTION TO ONE'S BODY
- CONNECTION TO ONE'S SELF
- CONNECTION TO OTHERS
- CONNECTION TO THE DIVINE/GOD
- COOLING
- CRAFTING
- CREATIVITY
- DANCING
- ENERGY
- FAT
- FEELING GOOD
- FEELING LIKE YOU'RE ENOUGH
- FOOD
- FRIENDSHIP
- GATHERING
- INTIMACY
- JOY
- JUST BEING
- LAUGHTER
- LEARNING/COMPREHENSION
- LETTING GO
- LOVE
- MEANING
- MOVEMENT
- MUSIC
- PERMISSION
- PLAY
- PROTEIN
- PURPOSE
- QUIET
- RECOGNITION/BEING SEEN
- RESTORATION
- RITUAL
- SALT
- SATIATION
- SECURITY/SAFETY
- SEX
- SINGING
- SPACIOUSNESS
- SPEAKING/COMMUNICATING
- STIMULATION
- STORYTELLING
- STRUCTURE
- TOUCH
- TRADITION
- TRUTH
- VITALITY
- WARMTH
- WATER
- WHITE SPACE

Secondary hungers are more specific and superficial. They point to a deeper, primary hunger. They can also be thought of as the *how* whereas the primary hunger is the *what*.

We want to feed our primary hunger through secondary hungers that are a good fit. When I was trying to feed my hunger for physical affection (a primary hunger) through eating a large pizza (a secondary hunger) it wasn't a good fit. I was never going to satisfy one with the other. If my primary hunger had been for warm food, carbohydrates, protein, or fat, eating pizza would have been a great match.

Here are a few more examples:

>SECONDARY HUNGER: *New red shoes*
>PRIMARY HUNGER: *Adventure*
>
>SECONDARY HUNGER: *Date night with significant other*
>PRIMARY HUNGER: *Physical affection*
>
>SECONDARY HUNGER: *To quit my job*
>PRIMARY HUNGER: *Meaningful work*

Using a primary and secondary hunger framework helps me, but it's not a science. It's just another tool to help us look deeper. Especially when we get hung up on not being able to fulfill a secondary hunger, realizing that we can feed the primary hunger in a different way frees us.

HOW DO I FEED MY HUNGERS? WHAT ACTIONS SHOULD I TAKE?

We'll talk more about this next week, but here's a start:

Make choices. Listen for feedback about what has and hasn't fed you. Take teeny tiny steps and occasionally, take a big step. Tell the people who care about you what you're hungry for. Feed yourself in small ways when your big hungers can't be fulfilled yet. Feed your primary hungers through whatever secondary hungers are possible, and are a good fit for you.

We're going to spend this week listening and applying what we've learned about self-compassion and intuitive eating to our non-food hungers.

SUMMARY

We've covered a lot in this lesson, so here's a recap:

1. Walking the path to becoming a well-fed woman is about adopting a new paradigm. It's not a flip we switch on, a quick fix, or a static place we arrive to where we're never hungry again.

2. To live a well-fed life is to be guided by four beliefs:

- *All of our hungers are wise. They form the internal compass that points us toward what we need.*
- *We are all equally worthy of being well-fed. No one is more or less worthy of having a well-fed life.*
- *When we're well-fed, we can be fully engaged and effective in life. Feeding ourselves is an act of service.*
- *A world full of well-fed people (especially women) is a better world.*

3. Well-fed women get hungry, feel pain, don't always know what they are hungry for, and don't always have an easy time feeding their hungers.

4. Being a well-fed woman is almost entirely about listening to your hungers and feeling worthy of what you need.

5. We have to quiet the need to know the *how* in order to create space to hear the what.

6. There are primary hungers and secondary hungers. When we peel back the layers of our secondary hungers, we discover our primary hunger and open new possibilities for how it might be fed.

WEEK TEN

BECOMING A WELL-FED WOMAN / WEEK TEN REFLECTIONS

Note: For the most part, over the next few weeks, when I talk about hungers I'm referring to non-food hungers.

COMPLETE THESE SENTENCES:

If there were no 'shoulds' and 'shouldnt's', the hunger of mine that I'd claim is:

I don't know how I could possibly feed this hunger, but the truth is I am hungry for:

I can tell that I'm not well-fed when:

Reflecting on the parallels between my relationship to food and my other life hungers, I can see that:

If I knew I only had one year to live, I'd make sure I was well-fed by _____

WEEK TEN

Begin to brainstorm and explore your own hungers through the lens of primary and secondary hungers. Remember, a secondary hunger is more on the surface and more specific. Primary hungers are more general, more universal, and exist at the root of our secondary hungers. A few examples:

SECONDARY HUNGER:
New red shoes

SECONDARY HUNGER:
Date night with my husband

SECONDARY HUNGER:
To quit my job

PRIMARY HUNGER:
Adventure

PRIMARY HUNGER:
Physical affection

PRIMARY HUNGER:
Meaningful work

This is just a brainstorming exercise, so if you're not sure, or only a few come to mind, that's totally okay. We're still just opening up to this question.

SECONDARY HUNGERS	PRIMARY HUNGERS

Each of us has beliefs and stories that, while not true, hold a great deal of power. The first step to a story becoming less powerful is simply naming it. Use this space to reflect on any beliefs or stories you have that might be standing in between you and naming or feeding your hungers.

Each slice of this wheel represents a core area of your life. If you want to add to or edit these eight areas, feel free.

Your task is to shade in from the center point outward in each slice how well-fed you feel in each area. If you don't feel well-fed at all the slice will hardly be shaded in at all. If you feel very well-fed the slice may be shaded in almost completely. As you do this you'll notice that some areas of your life (and you) are well-fed while others are less so.

Once you've completed your Wheel of Life, simply notice and reflect on what you see. How might this exercise help you live a more well-fed life?

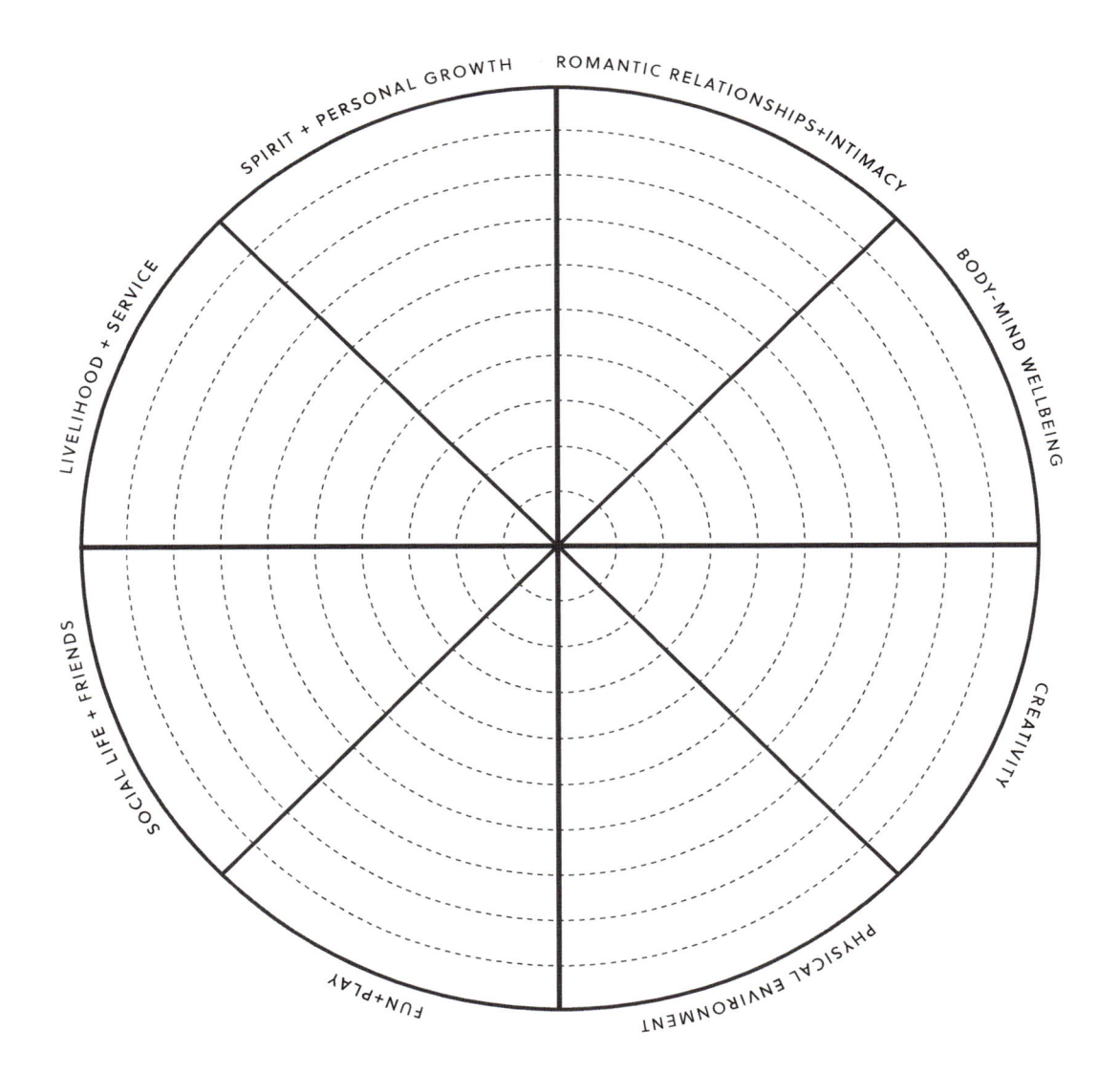

WEEK TEN

BECOMING A WELL-FED WOMAN / WEEK TEN CHALLENGES

Use this space to write a letter to yourself from your non-food hungers that you identified yesterday. Give them a voice. Let them speak their truth. If you get stuck, use the prompt *"What I really want to say is…"*

Make a date this week or weekend to have a conversation with someone in your life about your (and their) hungers. Pick someone who's kind and supportive. It can be a girlfriend, your life partner, or someone in the *Feast* group. Try to stay away from talking about your hunger(s) like problems to fix and instead approach the topic from a place of wonder, hope, possibility, curiosity, kindness, and honesty. This challenge might seem easy to skip, life is busy after all, but we don't talk about hungers very often and I want to encourage you to change that.

RESOURCE FOLDER INTERVIEWEES

Susannah Conway

Susannah Conway is the author of *This I Know: Notes on Unraveling the Heart* (Skirt! Books) and forthcoming *LONDONTOWN: A Photographic Tour of the City's Delights* (Chronicle Books, Spring 2016).
A photographer, writer and teacher, her classes have been enjoyed by thousands of people from over 50 countries around the world. Co-author of *Instant Love: How to Make Magic and Memories with Polaroids* (Chronicle Books), Susannah helps others remember their true selves, using creativity as the key to open the door. Visit her at *SusannahConway.com*.

Julie Daley

Julie Daley is an educator, consultant, and transformational coach who brings the kind of personal and organizational growth so needed in our world today. She's worked with people from around the world and all walks of life to guide them to discover and uncover their personal creativity and essential nature. After working with Julie, you will find you'll be better able to bring out both, providing a firm foundation for all you wish to create and do in your life. Julie offers one-on-one coaching, courses, consulting in areas of personal creativity, compassion, and authentic leadership, and speaks on a range of topics in these areas. Julie offers practical wisdom and deep insight for how you can engage more of your essential nature in all that you long to do and create in your life. Learn more about Julie at *unabashedlyfemale.com*.

WEEK TEN

Vivienne McMaster

Vivienne McMaster is a photographer, workshop leader and positive body image advocate from Vancouver, Canada. She who helps folks around the world see themselves with compassion through their own camera lens. Her photographs have been seen in such places as Oprah.com and the The Huffington Post. The camera and self-portraiture helped her heal her own negative body image and she's now on a mission share these tools and help women choose compassion over critique, one photo at a time. You can more learn about her at *beyourownbeloved.com*.

Rachelle Mee-Chapman

Rachelle Mee-Chapman is a former evangelical minister who left the church when it's practices became out of alignment with her core values and convictions. Now she is a life coach and spiritual director, working with clients who self-describe as post-church, formerly churched, unchurched, and spiritual but not religious. She considers herself a hostess -- holding space to help people curate their religious past and craft their relig-ish future. She hosts Flock, an online community for women that together have created a rotating set of practices that let us live-out our core values in simple, everyday ways. She is currently writing her book *Becoming Relig-ish*. Learn more about Rachelle at *magpie-girl.com*.

Juna Mustad

Juna Mustad is a Life & Relationship Coach, as well as an Intuitive. In her work, she uses a skillful combination of intuition, the Hendricks Institute's brilliant whole-body coaching techniques, and somatic therapy. She has a deep passion for supporting others in having healthy relationships, as well as emotionally intelligent lives. This is illustrated in her workshops and her relationship blog - with over 100 free relationship videos. Learn more at *JunaMustad.com* and *DailyRelationship.com*.

Kira Sabin

Kira Sabin has been coaching single men and women from San Diego to Singapore since 2007. She is a professionally certified coach through the International Coach Academy and a member of the International Coaching Federation. She has been a source and contributor for *Huffington Post*, *USA Today*, *Your Tango*, *Yahoo Shine*, *Chicago Tribune*, *The Frisky* and *Divine Caroline*. In 2010, she created the blog TheCollegeCrush.com to give Gen Y healthy dating and relationship advice and have become a national college speaker on the subject of dating with technology. She now writes and coaches over at *starttravelinglight.com*.

WEEK TEN

Laura Simms

Laura Simms is an expert on meaningful work who challenges conventional wisdom by asking people to ditch their passions and start with purpose. After struggling through her own career transition, Laura developed Your Career Homecoming, her signature career change process, to help people find careers that feel like home. Over 60 websites, podcasts, and universities have turned to Laura for career advice, including *US News & World Report*, The Huffington Post, and The University of California, Irvine. Working with clients internationally, Laura is proving that the purpose-driven approach leads to meaningful, profitable careers. She reluctantly lives in Texas and loves spending time on the front porch with her husband, son, friends, and guitar. Learn more about Laura at *withlaurasimms.com*.

Bari Tessler

Bari Tessler Linden, MA, is a Financial Therapist, Mentor Coach and Mama-preneur. Bari's gentle, body-centered approach weaves together personal, couple, and creative entrepreneurial money teachings into one complete tapestry. She is the founder of The Art of Money: a global, year-long money school, which integrates Money Healing, Money Practices and Money Maps. Bari is also the Author of her upcoming book, *The Art of Money: A Life-Changing Guide to Financial Happiness*, published by Parallax Press in Spring 2016. Learn more about Bari at *baritessler.com*.

Michelle Ward

Michelle Ward, PCC, has been offering dream career guidance for creative women as The When I Grow Up Coach since 2008. You may have seen or heard her in *New York Magazine*, *The Huffington Post*, *Etsy*, *Newsweek*, *Freelancers Union*, the *Forbes* Top 100 Websites for your Career List or 100+ other media outlets. She's the co-author of The Declaration of You, which was published by North Light Books, and the teacher of *Create Your Dream Career and Ditch Your Day Job*, which were watched by tens of thousands of people live on CreativeLive. Discover and achieve your dream career at *www.whenigrowupcoach.com*.

Chris Zydel

Chris Zydel, AKA the Wild Heart Queen, is head creative goddess at Creative Juices Arts. She has over 38 years of experience as a compassionate creativity guide. As a creativity coach Chris has successfully mentored countless writers, painters, photographers and business owners, and anyone with a creative vision trying to be born. She also performs this magic through her Painting From *The Wild Heart* workshops, training programs and retreats, providing nurturing and joy-filled creative sanctuaries overflowing with encouragement, permission and trust in the sacred energy of play and creativity that lives inside of us all. Visit her at *creativejuicesarts.com*.

WEEK TEN

NOTES

NOTES

WEEK TEN

DAILY PRACTICE CHECKLIST

GENERAL *FEAST* SKILLS	S 10/2	M 10/3	T 10/4	W 10/5	Th 10/6	F 10/7	Sa 10/8
Meditated (on own or with recording)							
Read Feast Material							
Wrote responses to reflection questions							
Listened to expert interview/live call							
Reached out to the group for support							
Meditated (on own or with recording)							
Meditated (on own or with recording)							

SELF-COMPASSION SKILLS	S 10/2	M 10/3	T 10/4	W 10/5	Th 10/6	F 10/7	Sa 10/8
Spoke kindly to myself							
Acted self-compassionately toward myself							

CARE FOR SENSITIVE SOUL SKILLS	S 10/2	M 10/3	T 10/4	W 10/5	Th 10/6	F 10/7	Sa 10/8
Attempted to mangage my sensory input							
Advocated for my HSP needs							
Celebrated/observed my HSP strengths							

EFFECTIVE EMOTIONAL COPING SKILLS	S 10/2	M 10/3	T 10/4	W 10/5	Th 10/6	F 10/7	Sa 10/8
Paused!							
RAIN (recognize, allow, investigate, natural awareness)							
Made a concious choice to distract							
Urge surfed							
Reached out to the group for support							
Did cost/benefit analysis							
Went in slo-mo							

WEEK TEN

HUNGER/FULLNESS SKILLS	S 10/2	M 10/3	T 10/4	W 10/5	Th 10/6	F 10/7	Sa 10/8
Recognized bodily cues re: hunger/fullness							
Honored bodily cues re: hunger/fullness							
Used the hunger-fullness scale							
Ate when I was hungry (before starving)							
Stopped when I was satisfied (before stuffed)							

EATING FREELY SKILLS	S 10/2	M 10/3	T 10/4	W 10/5	Th 10/6	F 10/7	Sa 10/8
Turned away from nutrition noise and toward my inner wisdom							
Made food choices for reasons beyond nutrition or health							
Made choices, rather than deferred to 'shoulds' or 'shouldnt's'							
Challenged the good/bad label I once placed on food(s)							

PLEASURE & SATISFACTION SKILLS	S 10/2	M 10/3	T 10/4	W 10/5	Th 10/6	F 10/7	Sa 10/8
I chose to do/eat/receive something because it would give me pleasure							
I chose to do/eat/receive for pleasure without having to earn it or feel guilty							
I paid attention what I was doing/eating/receiving so as to maximize my pleasure							
I experienced the connection between pleasurable eating and feeling physically satisfied/full							

JOYFUL MOVEMENT SKILLS	S 10/2	M 10/3	T 10/4	W 10/5	Th 10/6	F 10/7	Sa 10/8
I moved my body in some way that felt good/joyful/pleasurable to my body							
I rested my body when it requested rest							
I released old thoughts of exercising for punishment or as a means to earn the right to eat more							
I released self-judgement about what others might think of my body when I'm joyfully moving							

WEEK TEN

BECOMING A WELL-FED WOMAN SKILLS	S 10/2	M 10/3	T 10/4	W 10/5	Th 10/6	F 10/7	Sa 10/8
Asked myself 'What are you truly hungry for?'							
Allowed myself to name/feel a hunger without pressure to take any action, fix, or solve							
Made a request to someone to help feed a hunger of mine							
Honored a boundary (said 'no') to help myself be well-fed							
Took action to feed a non-food hunger							

WEEK ELEVEN

Becoming a Well-fed Woman

Part II

LIVING A WELL-FED LIFE

Genius is one percent inspiration and ninety-nine percent perspiration

THOMAS EDISON

When it comes to taking action and making change in our lives, a lot of people live by Nike's motto, "Just do it." While there are some occasions where this fairly unforgiving directive comes in handy, it can leave us with more guilt and shame because we can't always, "just do it." Change makes us vulnerable. There is nothing safe or secure about change, even if it is in the direction of what feeds us, and away from what leaves us hungry. Change can be scary. It can make our minds quick to chatter:

> WHAT IF I HURT SOMEONE?
> WHAT IF I WANT TOO MUCH?
> WHAT IF I FAIL?
> WHAT IF WHAT I HUNGER FOR ISN'T POSSIBLE?
> SHOULDN'T I JUST BE GRATEFUL FOR WHAT I ALREADY HAVE?

In the face of taking action that scares me, "just do it" falls short. I prefer the formula: 99% percent inspiration + 1% percent perspiration = my hunger is fed.

7 INGREDIENTS FOR INSPIRATION

Inspiration is the fertile soil from which our feast will grow. You already have many of the ingredients that make up the rich loam of inspiration.

1. SELF-COMPASSION

Taking action to feed yourself is much easier when you give yourself permission to be human, messy and imperfect, and make a commitment to meet yourself, as often as possible, with kindness.

2. DEVOTION TO THE FOUR WELL-FED WOMAN BELIEFS

When you dedicate your life to the beliefs that all of our hungers are wise, that we are all equally worthy of being well-fed, that being well-fed allows us to be fully engaged and effective in life, and that a world full of well-fed people is a better world, your next steps will follow.

3. REVERENCE FOR YOUR FEEDBACK LOOP

Anytime we do anything, we experience feedback from our body about whether it was a positive, neutral, or negative experience. With just one bite of food, we can know whether we want more or not. After one date, we can know if we want a second. Utilizing our feedback loop is essential to taking action to feed our hungers. Becoming a well-fed woman is a process of trial and error. The more we can embrace this process by tasting as many of life's offerings as possible, the more likely we'll know what our next step is.

4. APPRECIATION OF WHO YOU REALLY ARE

There is no right way to live, despite what anyone (especially our inner critic) has to say about it. There is no right way to look, eat, dress, have sex, learn, have fun, spend money, spend time, or even sleep. When we're stuck in self-judgment, it can be difficult to move towards fulfilling our true hungers. Let go of all of your "shoulds" and embrace who you really are.

5. ACCEPTANCE OF YOUR MANY NEEDS

It's pretty hard to feed our hungers when we're trying to keep them small and convenient. The bottom line is that humans have lots of hungers, and big ones; unfortunately, many women have been taught not to have hungers. If you want to feast on your life, then give up trying to be an air plant that lives without soil and can survive for long periods of drought. Instead, start soaking up as much soil, sun, and rain as you need to grow into a strong and healthy plant. Only you and your body know how much and just which nutrients (food and non-food) are required. It's okay to need and want a lot. What matters is that you become the fullest expression of you.

6. FREEDOM FROM YOUR TIMETABLE

It's easier to feed your hungers when you let go of your mental timetable ("I should have figured this out earlier in life") and the idea that you're somehow late ("No one my age finds a new career"). These are just stories that impede the actions that will carry you to your well-fed life. Without these stories you are free to meet yourself wherever you are on your winding path and in your own time. When you let go of a timetable, you can focus on this moment, rather than become overwhelmed with the big picture, or some artificial deadline ("I have to find love before I turn 40"). Repeat after me: There is no timetable. There is no right order of events. There is no deadline. I am not late.

7. BASIC SELF-CARE PRACTICE

Basic self-care goes a long way. As *Feast* has hopefully helped you to understand, management of our emotions, care of our highly sensitive temperaments, and regularly eating foods that feel and taste good all add up to our being on more stable ground to feed our hungers.

Take a moment to reflect on how the seven ingredients for inspiration show up in your own life:

1. SELF-COMPASSION
2. DEVOTION TO THE FOUR WELL-FED WOMAN BELIEFS
3. REVERENCE FOR YOUR FEEDBACK LOOP
4. APPRECIATION OF WHO YOU REALLY ARE
5. ACCEPTANCE OF YOUR MANY NEEDS
6. FREEDOM FROM YOUR TIMETABLE
7. BASIC SELF-CARE PRACTICE

Is there an ingredient asking for your attention? Is there an ingredient that comes more easily now than ten weeks ago?

I bet you're doing even better than you think!

PERSPIRATION

Perspiration is where the rubber meets the road. You've prepared the fertile ground of inspiration and you're ready to plant your seeds. Now what?

Now you make a choice. Then another. And another.

Instead of rebelling, or numbing out, you notice how much friendlier your life is as a Well-fed Woman, and you make a choice. Many of your choices will be tiny. Tiny is good. Tiny gets you places. And sometimes, once in awhile, you'll make a big choice.

YOU'LL MAKE THE CHOICE TO NAME YOUR HUNGER OUT LOUD.

You'll share your hunger with your partner and your best friend.

You'll tell anyone who asks, "How are you?" that you're moving in the direction of your hunger.

You'll ask for help, because none of us can become well-fed women on our own.

You'll make a point to take in, digest, and absorb whatever nourishment is right in front of you.

You'll feed your hunger in whatever imperfect way is available to you.

The exact steps you'll take will be based on your hunger, how ready you are to take action, how willing you are to have that step be imperfect, and what's going on in your life right now. Depending on your particular hunger, you might choose to read a book or take a course, hire a coach or find a buddy to take a dance class with, make a standing date night or set up a sacred nap time each afternoon.

The action part of feasting is simply this: **MAKE A CHOICE THAT FEELS ALIGNED WITH YOUR CURRENT HUNGER OR HUNGERS. DO NOT WAIT FOR PERFECTION.**

This week is all about beginning to take a few steps more in the direction of feeding yourself. If moving towards a particular hunger feels intimidating, take a step towards an easier one. Remember, taking action should be pleasurable, even if it's a bit scary.

Over the past ten weeks, you have prepared your fertile soil (your inspiration) so that when you take action (your perspiration) it doesn't feel so daunting. You've cleared the clutter and the noise, bridged the gaps, and come home to yourself.

Now you are free to choose.

WEEK ELEVEN

BECOMING A WELL-FED WOMAN / WEEK ELEVEN REFLECTIONS

Brainstorm time again. What is a small action step you could take today to move you closer to feeding one or more of your hungers? A prompt that might get you going is: *Today, to feed my hunger for* _____ *even a little, I could* _____ .

What request could you make of another to help feed one (or more) of your hungers? We often have a much easier time if we don't have to 'bother' someone else with our needs and wants. Well, we're not air plants. We have needs and we depend on each other to be well-fed. Practice writing here some things you'd like to request in your efforts to be more well-fed. Be specific.

Related to this, if it helps, reflect on the ways that your being well-fed serves others. Can you make the connection between you getting 'full' and other people benefitting? If so, explore that here:

BECOMING A WELL-FED WOMAN / WEEK ELEVEN CHALLENGES

This week is all about feeding yourself. Yes at the table, but especially away. This about taking action to step into a more well-fed version of yourself and your life. The action doesn't have to be big but your challenge is to do something that moves you in the direction of well-fed. Use this space to reflect on what baby steps you can begin to take.

This is our final week of *Feast* before next week's wrap-up. Is there anything you want to say, do, ask, write, read, etc before we're done? If so, your challenge is to seize the day and do it! Use this space to capture anything on your *Feast* to-do list.

WEEK ELEVEN

NOTES

Want more?

Then check out these related posts that Rachel has written.

ETERNAL SPRING
http://goo.gl/RB2fWP

THE COURAGE TO FEED YOUR TRUE HUNGERS
http://goo.gl/IbNgAf

PRIMARY HUNGERS
http://goo.gl/4EtvNC

HUNGRY FOR THE IMPOSSIBLE
http://goo.gl/qVx0CF

FOUR HUNGER RELATIONSHIPS
http://goo.gl/tmPfs3

SEPARATION OF POWERS
http://goo.gl/atGHu9

NOTES

WEEK ELEVEN

NOTES

DAILY PRACTICE CHECKLIST

GENERAL *FEAST* SKILLS	S 10/9	M 10/10	T 10/11	W 10/12	Th 10/13	F 10/14	Sa 10/15
Meditated (on own or with recording)							
Read Feast Material							
Wrote responses to reflection questions							
Listened to expert interview/live call							
Reached out to the group for support							
Meditated (on own or with recording)							
Meditated (on own or with recording)							

SELF-COMPASSION SKILLS	S 10/2	M 10/10	T 10/11	W 10/12	Th 10/13	F 10/14	Sa 10/15
Spoke kindly to myself							
Acted self-compassionately toward myself							

WEEK ELEVEN

CARE FOR SENSITIVE SOUL SKILLS	S 10/2	M 10/10	T 10/11	W 10/12	Th 10/13	F 10/14	Sa 10/15
Attempted to mangage my sensory input							
Advocated for my HSP needs							
Celebrated/observed my HSP strengths							

EFFECTIVE EMOTIONAL COPING SKILLS	S 10/2	M 10/10	T 10/11	W 10/12	Th 10/13	F 10/14	Sa 10/15
Paused!							
RAIN (recognize, allow, investigate, natural awareness)							
Made a concious choice to distract							
Urge surfed							
Reached out to the group for support							
Did cost/benefit analysis							
Went in slo-mo							

HUNGER/FULLNESS SKILLS	S 10/2	M 10/10	T 10/11	W 10/12	Th 10/13	F 10/14	Sa 10/15
Recognized bodily cues re: hunger/fullness							
Honored bodily cues re: hunger/fullness							
Used the hunger-fullness scale							
Ate when I was hungry (before starving)							
Stopped when I was satisfied (before stuffed)							

EATING FREELY SKILLS	S 10/2	M 10/10	T 10/11	W 10/12	Th 10/13	F 10/14	Sa 10/15
Turned away from nutrition noise and toward my inner wisdom							
Made food choices for reasons beyond nutrition or health							
Made choices, rather than deferred to 'shoulds' or 'shouldnt's'							
Challenged the good/bad label I once placed on food(s)							

WEEK ELEVEN

PLEASURE & SATISFACTION SKILLS	S 10/2	M 10/10	T 10/11	W 10/5	Th 10/13	F 10/14	Sa 10/15
I chose to do/eat/receive something because it would give me pleasure							
I chose to do/eat/receive for pleasure without having to earn it or feel guilty							
I paid attention what I was doing/eating/receiving so as to maximize my pleasure							
I experienced the connection between pleasurable eating and feeling physically satisfied/full							

JOYFUL MOVEMENT SKILLS	S 10/2	M 10/10	T 10/11	W 10/5	Th 10/13	F 10/14	Sa 10/15
I moved my body in some way that felt good/joyful/pleasurable to my body							
I rested my body when it requested rest							
I released old thoughts of exercising for punishment or as a means to earn the right to eat more							
I released self-judgement about what others might think of my body when I'm joyfully moving							

BECOMING A WELL-FED WOMAN SKILLS	S 10/2	M 10/10	T 10/11	W 10/5	Th 10/13	F 10/14	Sa 10/15
Asked myself 'What are you truly hungry for?' Sa 10/15							
Allowed myself to name/feel a hunger without pressure to take any action, fix, or solve							
Made a request to someone to help feed a hunger of mine							
Honored a boundary (said 'no') to help myself be well-fed							
Took action to feed a non-food hunger							

WEEK TWELVE

Closing, Celebration, and What's Next?

LIVING A WELL-FED LIFE

WE LOOK WITH UNCERTAINTY

We look with uncertainty
beyond the old choices for
clear-cut answers
to a softer, more permeable aliveness
which is every moment
at the brink of death;
for something new is being born in us
if we but let it.
We stand at a new doorway,
awaiting that which comes…
daring to be human creatures,
vulnerable to the beauty of existence.
Learning to love.

— ANNE HILLMAN

You did enough.

There is no more personal endeavor for me than *Feast*.

It includes (or at least I've tried to include) nearly every single "brick" I needed I build my own path out of hunger and misery. The awe I feel getting to offer to you the healing that has so revolutionized my life is immeasurable.

I can't help—when watching each of you softening your hearts, seeing how not alone you are, learning that starvation and cruelty do not have to be your reality, and most of all, stepping into your big, glorious power—but feel like all those hellish years of mine had some deeper meaning.

Lately, what I hear when I talk to each of you is that everyday I chose to embrace myself created a brighter, kinder world for you. I wonder if you can you see now that you do the same for me? Can you see that everyday you choose to love yourself the world I live in is a kinder, brighter place. You see we need each other in this way so profoundly.

I suppose this brings me to the larger mission of *Feast* and the third and fourth Well-fed Woman tenets:

#3 Well-fed women get hungry, feel pain, don't always know what they are hungry for, and don't always have an easy time feeding their hungers.

#4 Being a well-fed woman is almost entirely about listening to your hungers and feeling worthy of what you need.

When I encounter the problems of the world, and there are many, it only renews my commitment to this work and to you feasting on your life.

Please don't for one moment feel that you didn't do enough or learn enough in these past three months. It takes years and years to really embody these teachings. You're just 12 weeks in and from what I've witnessed you are well on your way. I don't see you through critical eyes though. I see you through eyes of love and hope that you can adopt these same lenses.

Hear me:

You did enough. More than enough.

You showed up enough. More than enough.

You, just by being you, in your process, in your own way were of service to the healing of the entire circle of *Feast* women. Feel this.

You learned what you needed to learn at this time and what you didn't learn remains here for you to practice, explore, and stumble through going forward.

Love,

Rachel

WEEK TWELVE

INTEGRATION & CLOSING / WEEK TWELVE REFLECTIONS

TAKING STOCK

Review each of *Feast*'s themes. What did you learn? What new skill or tool did you come away with? What questions do you still have?

SELF-COMPASSION

CARING FOR YOUR SENSITIVE SOUL

COPING EFFECTIVELY WITH EMOTIONS

HONORING HUNGER & FULLNESS

EATING FREELY

PLEASURE & SATISFACTION

JOYFUL MOVEMENT

BECOMING A WELL-FED WOMAN I & II

WEEK TWELVE

Complete these sentences:

When I first signed up for *Feast* I _____ and now I _____.

Looking back, I'd tell the pre-*Feast* me that…

When I look at myself, my life or the world around me post-*Feast*, I see things differently. For example:

Looking back over my *Feast* journey, I'm really proud of myself for….

LOOKING AHEAD

Your *Feast* journey doesn't end here. Use today's reflections to begin to get clear on what's next for you. With *Feast* coming to a close, the support I need going forward is:

EXAMPLES OF SUPPORT YOU MIGHT SEEK OUT INCLUDE:

- *Work with rachel 1:1*
- *Work with a therapist or other healer*
- *Work with an ie nutritionist*
- *Form an accountability partnership with another feast graduate*
- *Sign up to take feast again next round*
- *Read the book:*
- *Join/arrange/buy _____ for regular joyful movement.*

WEEK TWELVE

INTEGRATION & CLOSING / WEEK TWELVE CHALLENGES

1. Based on what you explored in yesterday's reflections, what action can you take today or this week to set up or confirm support going forward?

Your challenge is to do it. Make the call. Send the email. Book the appointment. Order the book. Reach out. Keep your momentum going!

2. Review the suggested reading list Rachel shared at the start of the course and consider diving into a new book to continue your learning.

3. Set up a celebratory meal with a friend(s), life partner, or even solo to acknowledge the journey you've just traveled, to punctuate this turning of the chapters, and to be seen by those who care about you.

You might just say: *"The past three months were kind of a big deal in my life. I kicked butt. It wasn't always easy. I'm wiser/happier/freer now and I want to celebrate! I want to Feast with you! Join me?"*

Aim to get this on the calendar in the next 3-5 days. :)

4. If you were to give yourself an award (any award) for the past three months, what award would you give yourself? For example *"The Brave Heart Award"* or *"Most Awakened"*. These are totally made up but give it a go and come share your award in the Facebook group!

WEEK TWELVE

SUGGESTED READING LIST

In addition to *Intuitive Eating: A Revolutionary Program that Works* by Evelyn Tribole and Elyse Resch (2012) the following books will greatly augment your learning.

WEEK ONE / SELF-COMPASSION

Self Compassion: The Proven Power of Being Kind to Yourself by Kristin Neff (2011)

The Gifts of Imperfection: Let Go of Who You Think You're Supposed to Be and Embrace Who You Are by Brené Brown (201)

There is Nothing Wrong with You: Going Beyond Self-Hatred by Cheri Huber (2001)

Radical Acceptance: Embracing Your Life With the Heart of a Buddha by Tara Brach (2004)

WEEK TWO / CARING FOR THE SENSITIVE SOUL

The Highly Sensitive Person: How to Thrive When the World Overwhelms You by Elaine Aron (1997)

Meditation Secrets for Women: Discovering Your Passion, Pleasure, and Inner Peace by Camille Morin and Lorin Roche (2001)

Sabbath: Finding Rest, Renewal, and Delight in our Busy Lives by Wayne Muller (2000)

WEEK THREE / EFFECTIVE EMOTIONAL COPING

End Emotional Eating: Using Dialectical Behavior Therapy Skills to Cope with Difficult Emotions and Develop a Healthy Relationship to Food by Jennifer Taitz (2012)

Broken Open: How Difficult Times Help Us Grow by Elizabeth Lesser (2005)

WEEK FIVE / HONORING HUNGER & FULLNESS

Women, Food, & God: An Unexpected Path to Almost Everything by Geneen Roth (2011)

Body Respect: What Conventional Health Books Get Wrong, Leave Out, and Just Plain Fail to Understand about Weight by Linda Bacon and Lucy Aphramor (2014)

WEEK SIX / EATING FREELY

Eat!: Rediscover Your Best Natural Relationship with Food by Linda Harper (2014)

Embody: Learning to Love Your Unique Body (and quiet that critical voice!) by Connie Sobczak (2014)

Big Girl: How I Gave Up Dieting and Got a Life by Kelsey Miller (2016)

WEEK SEVEN / PLEASURE & SATISFACTION

Appetites: Why Women Want by Caroline Knapp (2011)

A Life of Being, Having, and Doing Enough by Wayne Muller (2011)

Eating in the Light of the Moon: How Women Can Transform Their Relationship with Food Through Myths, Metaphors, and Storytelling by Anita Johnston (2000)

WEEK EIGHT / JOYFUL MOVEMENT

Yoga and Body Image: 25 Personal Stories About Beauty, Bravery & Loving Your Body edited by Melanie Klein and Anna Guest-Jelley (2014)

Somatics: Reawakening The Mind's Control Of Movement, Flexibility, And Health by Thomas Hanna (2004)

Sweat Your Prayers: Movement as a Spiritual Practice by Gabrielle Roth (1998)

WEEK TEN & ELEVEN / BECOMING A WELL-FED WOMAN

Finding Your Own North Star: Claiming the Life You Were Meant to Live by Martha Beck (2002)

The Purpose of Your Life: Finding Your Place In The World Using Synchronicity, Intuition, And Uncommon Sense by Carol Adrienne (1999)

Women Who Run with the Wolves by Clarissa Pinkola Estes (1996)

WEEK TWELVE

GOOD PEOPLE TO KNOW AND FOLLOW

BODY POSITIVE FOLKS AND ORGANIZATIONS

Adios Barbie
http://www.adiosbarbie.com

Anna Guest-Jelley/Curvy Yoga
www.curvyyoga.com

The Association for Size Diversity and Health (ASDAH)
www.sizediversityandhealth.org

Be Nourished
www.benourished.org

The Body Positive
www.thebodypositive.org

Carmen Cool
www.carmencool.com

Geneen Roth
www.geneenroth.com

Golda Poretsky
www.bodylovewellness.com

The Fuck It Diet & Caroline Dooner
www.thefuckitdiet.com

Isabel Foxen Duke
www.isabelfoxenduke.com

Jes Baker
www.themilitantbaker.com

Marilyn Wann
www.fatso.com

Melissa Fabello at Everyday Feminism
www.everydayfeminism.com/author/melissaf/

Virgie Tovar
www.virgietovar.com

Vivienne McMaster
www.beyourownbeloved.com

IE AND HAES-FRIENDLY NUTRITIONISTS

Aaron Flores
http://www.bvmrd.com

Soolman Nutrition
www.soolmannutrition.com

Karin Kratina
www.eatingwisdom.com

Tracy Brown
www.tracybrownrd.com

Minh-Hai Alex
www.mindfulnutritionseattle.com

MEDITATION TEACHERS

Cheri Huber
www.cherihuber.com

Susan Piver
www.susanpiver.com

James Baraz
www.awakeningjoy.info

Tara Brach
www.tarabrach.com

Pema Chodron
www.pemachodronfoundation.org

Wisdom Heart
www.wisdomheart.com

Sharon Salzberg
www.sharonsalzberg.com

DAILY PRACTICE CHECKLIST

GENERAL *FEAST* SKILLS	S	M	T	W	Th	F	Sa
Meditated (on own or with recording)							
Read Feast Material							
Wrote responses to reflection questions							
Listened to expert interview/live call							
Reached out to the group for support							
Meditated (on own or with recording)							
Meditated (on own or with recording)							

SELF-COMPASSION SKILLS	S	M	T	W	Th	F	Sa
Spoke kindly to myself							
Acted self-compassionately toward myself							

CARE FOR SENSITIVE SOUL SKILLS	S	M	T	W	Th	F	Sa
Attempted to mangage my sensory input							
Advocated for my HSP needs							
Celebrated/observed my HSP strengths							

EFFECTIVE EMOTIONAL COPING SKILLS	S	M	T	W	Th	F	Sa
Paused!							
RAIN (recognize, allow, investigate, natural awareness)							
Made a concious choice to distract							
Urge surfed							
Reached out to the group for support							
Did cost/benefit analysis							
Went in slo-mo							

HUNGER/FULLNESS SKILLS	S	M	T	W	Th	F	Sa
Recognized bodily cues re: hunger/fullness							
Honored bodily cues re: hunger/fullness							
Used the hunger-fullness scale							
Ate when I was hungry (before starving)							
Stopped when I was satisfied (before stuffed)							

EATING FREELY SKILLS	S	M	T	W	Th	F	Sa
Turned away from nutrition noise and toward my inner wisdom							
Made food choices for reasons beyond nutrition or health							
Made choices, rather than deferred to 'shoulds' or 'shouldnt's'							
Challenged the good/bad label I once placed on food(s)							

PLEASURE & SATISFACTION SKILLS	S	M	T	W	Th	F	Sa
I chose to do/eat/receive something because it would give me pleasure							
I chose to do/eat/receive for pleasure without having to earn it or feel guilty							
I paid attention what I was doing/eating/ receiving so as to maximize my pleasure							
I experienced the connection between pleasurable eating and feeling physically satisfied/full							

JOYFUL MOVEMENT SKILLS	S	M	T	W	Th	F	Sa
I moved my body in some way that felt good/joyful/pleasurable to my body							
I rested my body when it requested rest							
I released old thoughts of exercising for punishment or as a means to earn the right to eat more							
I released self-judgement about what others might think of my body when I'm joyfully moving							

BECOMING A WELL-FED WOMAN SKILLS	S	M	T	W	Th	F	Sa
Asked myself 'What are you truly hungry for?'							
Allowed myself to name/feel a hunger without pressure to take any action, fix, or solve							
Made a request to someone to help feed a hunger of mine							
Honored a boundary (said 'no') to help myself be well-fed							
Took action to feed a non-food hunger							

Rachel Cole is a certified life coach, celebrated teacher, and women's empowerment expert.

She has spent ten years guiding women to identify, understand and feed their truest hungers – at and away from the table. As an eating disorder survivor herself, Rachel speaks with great wisdom, sensitivity, and authority about what it takes to live as a Well-fed Woman in the modern world. She has traveled across the United States and internationally speaking and teaching to sold-out gatherings of women on how they too can find ease and fulfillment in their lives simply by honoring their own hungers. As the founder of the popular biannual *Feast* program, Rachel leads intimate groups of women through a transformational three-month online masterclass on self-compassion, intuitive eating, and living life as a Well-fed Woman. She holds a Masters Degree in Holistic Health Education and is a Certified Professional Co-Active Coach.

You can learn more about Rachel and her work by visiting *rachelwcole.com* and following her at *facebook.com/feedyourlife* and *instagram.com/rachelwcole*.